Peter Wildblood is a management consultant and trainer. His
business is dedicated to improving performance in individuals
and organisations. He lives and works on Dangar Island in the
Hawkesbury River north of Sydney.

LEADING FROM WITHIN

■ Creating vision ■ Leading
change ■ Getting results

Peter Wildblood

ALLEN & UNWIN

Illustrations by Valda Brook

First published in 1995
Allen & Unwin Pty Ltd
9 Atchison Street, St Leonards, NSW 2065 Australia
Phone: (61 2) 9901 4088
Fax: (61 2) 9906 2218
E-mail: 100252.103@compuserve.com

National Library of Australia
Cataloguing-in-Publication entry:

Wildblood, Peter James.
  Leading from within: creating vision, leading change,
  getting results.

  Includes index.
  ISBN 1 86373 821 5.

  1. Leadership. 2. Creative ability in business.
  3. Success in business. I. Title.

650.1

Set in 10/11.5 pt Palatino by DOCUPRO, Sydney
Printed by SRM Production Services Sdn Bhd, Malaysia

10 9 8 7 6 5 4 3 2

Educare (Latin) — to lead forth from within

. . . the mythical Greek image of Scylla, the rock, and Charybdis, the whirlpool, which Odysseus and his sailors had to steer between, . . . characterize the hard and soft features of organizations, the structured, controlled, masculine side and the flexible, responsive feminine side, both of which are needed for success.

Charles Handy, *The Age of Paradox*

Foreword

The search for understanding of personal and organisational effectiveness and success is an old and worthy quest. The outcomes of the search are like pieces of a jig-saw puzzle. Some parts of the picture fit together with logic and harmony. Other parts of the picture have pieces missing and there are still lots of pieces that we don't know how or where to fit together. But the core elements of personal and organisational effectiveness are well understood and, perhaps not surprisingly, remarkably similar.

Organisations, like individuals, need to be *purposeful* to be successful. Purpose can be expressed in terms of a vision, an intent, or long-term aspirations complemented by short-term goals that, when achieved, give a sense of accomplishment and progress.

Organisations, like individuals, need *plans* on clearly defined courses of action that are goal related and practical. *Values* and *beliefs* in turn can provide consistency of action. And both organisations and individuals need *internal consistency*, a sense of integration that provides congruence and integrity.

Peter Wildblood has distilled the essence of personal and managerial effectiveness in a lucid, coherent and practical book that will lead its readers to exert greater influence initially over their own success and satisfaction, and then over the achievements and contributions of others.

In unfolding his logic, Peter not only revisits some of the well-established wisdom, but also adds new insights that will stimulate and inspire the reader to action. His underlying theme is that we are responsible for our own behaviour and its outcomes. Our destiny therefore lies largely within our own control: effectiveness, success and satisfaction can be created and multiplied as we work with and through others.

In one sense Peter's themes and analysis are timeless. Yet, in a world that is characterised by both increased complexity and interdependency, his ideas are more relevant each day.

I commend this book to you as both a stimulus and a guide to action. It represents a unique resource for enhancing our most precious personal asset: our self efficacy.

Roger Collins
Professor of Management
Australian Graduate School of Management

Contents

Acknowledgements

I owe a great debt to the countless people who have touched me in my personal, educational, social, sporting and business life over the years. Many of the names of these people now escape me and yet their contribution to me has been so considerable. Much of my greatest learning has come from the small proportion of them with whom I had some form of conflict.

Over the past ten years or so, as I have become more confident about my direction, I have exposed my ideas and experiences to those who have attended my seminars and workshops. For their involvement in the further development of my thoughts I owe a special vote of thanks.

A number of people have helped me directly in the years in which I have nurtured this book. Roger Collins was kind enough to cast a critical eye over an early draft. More recently Bob Henry, Michelle Stern, Richard Morcom and Adele Mitchell gave invaluable advice and assistance. Tom Miller spent many hours rehearsing his own colourful version of Albert Ellis's work here in my island paradise in 1992. Mark Tredinnick of Allen & Unwin gave a great deal of creative and personal encouragement at a critical stage; Rebecca Kaiser was a delight to work with in bringing the book from manuscript to publication.

To Paul Flotman and Sherry Stumm I owe a special debt. Both have spent more time and energy on focusing my ideas and experiences into words than I could have believed possible. The word 'friendship' takes on a whole new meaning for me as I contemplate their contribution.

To you all, I say 'Thank you!'

For the final result of all this wonderful support and encouragement I am happy to take full responsibility.

Introduction

As the business world moves into the 21st century, businesses of all sizes are undergoing a radical re-examination. The value of the 'front line' is receiving more and more emphasis. Middle management ranks are diminishing in number, if not disappearing entirely as organisations become flatter. 'Quality' is the *sina qua non* of personal and organisational success—the basis of client or customer satisfaction and of competitive advantage.

People with vision and the capacity to draw colleagues with them in a unified, commonly agreed direction are in greater demand than those people possessing only technical skills. At no time before has it been more important for people working in organisations to possess the twin skills essential to personal success: the technical skills required by their own position, and the relationship skills necessary for harnessing the creative energies of their colleagues.

Leading from Within reflects many years of experience, a great deal of research, and significant personal achievement by the author as a manager and consultant in a wide range of different work environments in the public and private sectors. For many years the essence of my experience has been presented to hundreds of people in seminars and workshops. This book is both the fruit of this experience and the culmination of a growing sense of frustration!

Management journals and bookshops are full of articles and books about 'new' and exciting ways to make a difference at a personal and organisational level; to bring organisations and the people in them to levels of performance appropriate to the demands of the global market and the accelerating rate of change in which we operate. 'Management by objectives' and 'clerical work management' are now *passé*. 'Total quality management' and 'total quality service' jockey for prominence with 'excellence' and 'empowerment'. And as they begin to wane in popularity, 'credibility' and 'the learning organisation' vie with 'international best practice' and 'business process re-engineering' for the attention of chief executives, while their people look on in bemusement.

My frustration stems not just from the plethora of 'answers' we are being offered; it also derives from my work as a consultant and trainer, and from my impressions as a senior manager. Whenever I talk in detail with the grassroots people in organisations, three common concerns spring to the fore, irrespective of the size or nature of the organisation:

- I have a strong feeling that this organisation does not have any real sense of direction.
- The senior people in my organisation do not seem to want to involve me in the decision-making process.
- I put a lot of extra effort into my job to make things work and no one seems to notice, much less acknowledge or thank me for what I do.

Managers of organisations seem to concentrate on the material needs of their role and ignore, or minimise, the importance people play in achieving objectives. Bottom-line results, cashflow, return on investment, inventory control, marketing, sales, product development and investment ratios are all essential elements of effective management. None of them can be achieved without the people of the organisation.

Organisations tend to reward performance, and promote people according to their technical skills rather than their skills in harnessing the energies of other people. Both are equally important.

As long ago as 1926, Henry Ford[1] included 'consider your customers' needs first', 'integrate change into your corporate culture', 'incorporate continuous improvement into design and manufacturing operations',[2] 'treat dealers and suppliers as partners', 'use just-in-time inventory management', and 'comprehensive employee training' in his list of principles that would create corporate success. He knew that the balance between technical and people management was critical to success.

So why are we still learning the same lesson? Our obsession with the more readily quantifiable, our penchant for dealing with people as objects (human resources), the growing complexity of our environment on this planet and the rate of change—particularly the speed with which we process 'information'—all spring to mind as possible answers.

To the increasing credit of our times, much of what is required—refocusing on the needs of the people in organisations—is being addressed in the current management literature. The signs are, however, that the gap between perceived need and practice is as wide, if not wider, than ever. The few who do something about it are far outweighed by both those who do not and those new entrants who have not even thought about the issue.

There are still changes occurring within organisations without consideration being given to the needs of the people until after the event, if at all. It is a rare merger or acquisition that gives equal weight to people and to financial issues.

There are still major programs of activity that are directed exclusively from the boardroom or the chief executive's suite without any involvement from the individuals who make up the cutting edge of those organisations. It is little wonder that institutional inertia is so strong and that change is resisted, when the needs of the people who will put the change into effect are almost totally ignored.

This book has been written, therefore, to support people in organisations to establish, develop and maintain:

- the skills of relationships with colleagues;
- an understanding of the nature of change and what it takes to encourage an ongoing commitment to change in a positive creative way; and
- the skills of personal organisation in support of other roles.

It has also been written on the premise that there is little of value not already known through your direct experience, whether it be positive or negative.

A number of basic premises that underpin human performance are presented in a way that will stimulate you to look at them anew for the value they represent in the 'new organisation' of the 21st century. In doing so, you will become more powerful in creating a positive effect on your own performance and more able to influence your work colleagues to mutual advantage, despite any apparent constraints within your work environment.

Too often we hold on to old familiar practices and blame the organisation and the people around us for failure to achieve our potential. Through a new look at these basic understandings of human performance, this book will give you the opportunity to rediscover your own worth and to explore the capacity you already have to really make things happen.

Leading from Within is designed to heighten your awareness of your abilities, as well as to present action strategies for improved performance. It is full of specific ideas, techniques and practices for improved performance for people aspiring to leadership; there is much in it for those already in a leadership position. It is not intended, however, that you should apply each and every idea presented. There are very few people, including myself, who do so. My purpose is to present a smorgasbord of ideas from which you may choose. This will translate into something of value for you in your work place and in those important groups of people called family, community and social and sporting associations.

If you want to rise to the challenge of the 'new organisation' and improve your performance to match the expectations and demands of the 21st century, some of your behaviour patterns and approaches of the past will have to change. Doing things differently from the way you have always done them can cause some underlying anxiety. This anxiety is often likely to drive you very creatively back to where you were. On the other hand, a determination to perform at a higher level will carry you through. Remember, the rewards in personal and organisational terms can be enormous.

Indeed there is, in each of us, the capacity to achieve things which are beyond our wildest dreams. All we need is to be very clear about what we wish to create in our lives and how to free ourselves in order to tap into the resources we possess. This book provides a key to unlocking these resources—to lead from within. It provides a vehicle to begin a journey during which you will progressively unfold your potential and discover your real capacity. It is a wonderful journey on which to embark; I wish you well on it.

> *If you always do what you've always done,*
> *you'll always get what you've always got.*

Anon.

SECTION 1

Creating and maintaining focus in self and others

CHAPTER 1

Focused attention for personal success

If you don't know where you are going you probably won't get there!

Anon.

In picking up this book you have indicated that you have one of the major attributes of a high achiever: you have shown an openness to new ideas and an interest in, or a desire to reach for, higher levels of achievement and success. This is the hallmark of high performance people.

What you have already achieved has come about by being focused, in one way or another, on what is really important to you.

No doubt your parents and your early school environment placed conscious and subconscious expectations upon you. Your immediate family and the social, cultural and sporting groups in which you moved provided an additional stimulus for your ambition and achievements. Almost certainly your exposure to the print and electronic media will also have influenced your hopes and aspirations. Your work, particularly short-term routine work, will have attracted subconscious performance expectations.

All these 'environmental' factors have affected you in one way or another and enabled you to focus on what is important to you and on what you want to achieve in your lifetime. Within this focus, you may have written down a particular goal for several major activities; for other goals you may have developed a clear mental picture.

Many of us, however, do not find it easy to establish a clear goal structure for personal and business activities. We simply have an 'immediate' and temporary focus.

WHY FOCUS IS SO IMPORTANT

Nothing is more critical to the successful management of your time, and to your level of productivity and general all-round effectiveness, than a strong focus.

Being focused has an incredibly powerful motivational effect on human performance. A study over a twenty-year period of a group of graduates from the Harvard School of Business showed a very strong correlation between detailed, written down, goal structures and personal success.[1] The interesting discovery by the researchers was that only 3 per cent of the group studied set goals in this way. A further 10 per cent had a strong perception of what they wanted to achieve, whereas the remaining 87 per cent had no clear idea of what they ultimately wanted. The 10 per cent with a clear idea ended up 'comfortably well off' after twenty years. The remainder ranged from those who had 'to work in paid employment' to 'dependent on some form of family or community assistance'.

What we achieve, or what we think we are able to achieve, is strongly related in our minds to our attitudes about time. Many of us are in 'deficit' about time. As we become busier we tend to become chronically over-committed and rush from one crisis to another at work and at home. A common lament is 'there are not enough hours in the day', or 'I never seem to have enough time to do the things I want to do'.

'I haven't enough time . . .' is rarely more than an excuse. The real question is what we choose to do with our time. Not having enough time may be a clue that we are not properly focused and we are not making the most appropriate choices on the way to meeting our objectives.

The motivational force of being strongly focused cannot be over-emphasised. Motivation is, after all, essentially personal and internal, however much it may be affected by environmental factors. Being focused, with clear written goals, is the most important element in generating motivation in people who expect to be high performers.

The reason for this is that we humans are teleological[2] in nature. In essence this means that consciously or subconsciously we decide what we want to do before we take any action and then base subsequent activity on that decision. When there is no conscious focus we tend to drift from one momentary subconscious 'pull' to another, often at the whim of another person or an environmental factor. Then we become easily distracted from

4

what might otherwise be our main purpose. 'Drift' or lack of focus is, unhappily, quite commonplace and leads to a sense of failure or lack of fulfilment. Hence the experience of the 87 per cent of subjects in the Harvard study mentioned earlier.

Top athletes, business and community leaders—top performers generally—do not experience this sense of drift. They possess a strong sense of their own destiny. They have a commitment to a positive goal structure. They have a strong vision of what is important to them. They are in fact focused. However, it is always necessary to weigh the cost of achieving a goal in terms of finances, time, relationships, health, stress and any other matters important to you.

Top performers with this strong sense of what is really important to them are tapping into their teleological force, a natural energy or drive available to us all. This clear focus on goals or objectives channels our energies towards achievement.

Every now and then in my lifetime I have been distressed to learn of the terminal illness of a close friend. In many cases, medical advice had been offered on the possible time remaining for them. I have watched how each of my friends used their time. For some it was business as before. For others there was an unrewarding oscillation between resignation and hope. For one or two the illness provided a challenge to make changes and create a quality of life they had long sought without any real focus.[3]

More and more I ask myself why does it take this kind of threat to help people distinguish between quality of life and resignation? Why do we have to watch someone close to us go through a process such as this before we learn the same lesson, if we do so at all? Why do we spend so much of our lives less productively than we might, and then be unhappy about what we have achieved? Why does resignation and defeat feature so strongly in our underlying attitudes?

George Bernard Shaw once said 'I want to be thoroughly used up when I die . . .'. George Burns is said to have signed a ten-year movie contract on his 90th birthday, with two ten-year options. What wonderful personal commitments!

Time is the only resource we have completely at our disposal. Each moment of our life is so precious that it should be a fundamental tenet that we spend it precisely as we wish. This does not necessarily mean constant productive business activity. It might just as easily mean quality recreational or social activity, quality time devoted to your health and fitness, or choices about food intake and physical rest.

Focus does not necessarily mean serious dogged pursuit of particular objectives. Focusing on what you really want is exciting and fulfilling. True, there may be certain aspects of the pursuit of some goals that seem mundane and ordinary at the time. Above all, however, it is your responsibility to let the pursuit of goals and objectives be exciting, to let it be fun! After all, excitement and fun come from a certainty that you are doing something that you want to do. It does not come from the outcome itself. Indeed the kind of excitement I speak of is 'achievement neutral'. It comes out of being constantly aware that what you are doing contributes to your wellbeing in a significant way. It does not matter whether your focus is on being the wealthiest person in the world, or whether it is on producing the most exquisite doorknob in your neighbourhood. Excitement, and therefore, motivation is generated by the focused pursuit, not the achievement. Note, for example, how 'empty' some former world champion athletes feel without additional goals to maintain their commitment and enthusiasm. They can be as excited and joyous about minor achievements as they can be dispirited about past glories they cannot repeat.

Similarly it is not enough to be clear about what we do *not* want. This may be a motivational force in some circumstances, although it is rarely sustainable over prolonged periods of time. Fear of failure is much less potent a force, over time, than a forward-looking positive focus.

Being focused is therefore a positive, forward-looking activity. To tap into this life force, to optimise the energy and personal motivation for achievement, it is useful to commit our focus into some form of conscious written structure of goals and objectives.

The way I would like you to structure your focus is set out in the following sections. It consists of a number of elements: a vision or a set of personal lifetime goals; values; involving others in your goal; balance; personal goals and objectives; and specific action steps.[4]

The importance of committing your goal structure to paper cannot be emphasised too strongly. For a start, there is the evidence of the Harvard study mentioned earlier, the logic of the telic[5] or inner force inherent in a strong focus. The mere act of writing down a goal will lift your focus from the general to the specific and will clear your subconscious goals to allow you to concentrate on the conscious. It is such a powerful process that you will find, in many instances, the means by which to achieve it will materialise without significant conscious effort on your part.

Perhaps you might like to try this for yourself. Write down two or three goals that at this point are outside your reach. Do so without regard to the resources now at your disposal. Put the list away in a safe place and make an appointment with yourself to review it at some later appropriate time. My guess is that you will have achieved one or more of your goals and made substantial progress on the others.

The power of conscious goal setting goes beyond simple direction setting. It requires responsibility for the use you make of your time. Put simply, a conscious goal structure keeps you informed as to whether you are spending your time on what is important to you. When you allow yourself to be governed by a subconscious or external goal structure, you have no such measure of your effectiveness. You commit to things that are not important to you. You over-commit, procrastinate and ultimately, under-achieve.

VISION

Most organisations[6] or teams have what is termed a vision or mission—a statement of their essential purpose. The personal equivalent might be called a 'personal lifetime goal'. A personal lifetime goal forms a basic framework from which goal choices and the more detailed objectives and specific action steps flow.

When the lifetime goal, major goals, objectives and specific action steps all point in the same direction, the force behind the whole is greater than the sum of the parts. It is like a magnet whose force comes from the alignment of the molecules of iron in the one direction. Without this alignment or congruence the piece of iron is heavy and lifeless.

A hierarchical congruence such as this, with each level of the overall goal structure aligned in the same direction, increases the power of strong personal focus. This sense of focus gives increased clarity to decisions and to any choices presented in meeting specified objectives. This sense of focus also provides a certainty about direction, providing motivation to achieve and stability in changing external circumstances. Unacceptable levels of stress are minimised, as energies are focused on an understood purpose.

A personal lifetime goal does not have to be over-long or

over-complicated. Simplicity has its own virtue. It can be expressed in general material terms (money, fortune or property); in terms of human relationships; in terms of family or community service; and in personal terms (happiness or love).

My experience of setting personal lifetime goals has been quite remarkable. Several years ago I decided that what I wanted to do with my life was 'devote myself 100 per cent to a life of love, joy and happiness, and of dynamic growth and fulfilment; to use my energies in assisting in the growth of family, friends, and the people with whom I work'. This goal has been amended slightly from time to time as my self-awareness and experience has grown and developed. It is stable rather than static.

With my lifetime goal firmly fixed in my mind and written down in a few key places in order to remind me of it and its importance, decisions about my life and my career have become easier to make. Life flows for me in the direction I have created for myself.

Naturally, there are ups and downs. Life is like that! Overall, having a personal lifetime goal has radically improved my family life and, in particular, my relationship with my partner and my two children. It has sharpened my focus on my career, and given me a sense of purpose in most of the activities in which I engage. It has enabled me to make decisions on personal and business activity based on other than purely material considerations. It has worked creatively for me in aligning most of my energies for one main purpose. On occasion, when I become aware that I am 'off purpose', it has made my understanding of my position quickly obvious and rendered the transition back to 'purpose' relatively easy.

In addressing and defining a personal lifetime goal for the first time, you might consider asking the question 'Why do I want that?'. Keep asking the same question on successive attempts. When your answer indicates there is no further dimension to your goal, you are close to the fundamental statement of purpose you want. For example, your self-questioning might go like this:

VERSION 1: to be fabulously wealthy

Why do I want that?

VERSION 2: to provide for me and my family in retirement

Why do I want that?

VERSION 3: to be independent

Why do I want that?

VERSION 4: to be comfortable and secure in all financial circum-stances; to be free of financial worry

Why do I want that?

VERSION 5: to be comfortable and secure in all financial circum-stances; to be free of financial worry

Often this reduction results in a statement about personal security or happiness or contentment.

It may well be that doing this brings you to a conclusion that you are in the wrong job or business. It may tell you that your personal circumstances are not what you would really like them to be. It may also show you how to define more clearly what you want to do with your business and personal life. If so, you are well on the way to being more focused and more attuned to your real purpose, to improved performance and increased personal fulfilment. The extent to which your personal goal structure is achieved is directly related to its integrity—the honesty and open-ness with which the structure is articulated. It is also directly related to the integrity of your relationships with members of your family and colleagues who are affected by it.

Try writing your personal lifetime goals down on a small card. Keep it in your wallet or diary, or in some place where it is easily accessible to you on a regular basis. Once a week, sit in a quiet place where you will not be interrupted and look over the words you have written. Close your eyes and relax and bring the goals into your mind for a few seconds. This reinforces them in your mind so that, in a short time, they become an automatic uncon-scious measure against which you can judge any major decision you are about to take. Decisions become easier. Life 'fits' together in the context of your personal lifetime goals.

PERSONAL VALUES

People don't care what you know unless
they know that you care!

Anon.

9

You may find it of great value to write down a set of personal, or guiding, values for the conduct of your personal and business life. A personal lifetime goal sets out your overall direction in a very fundamental way. Personal values spell out the way you want to behave in achieving your goal. It is a personal code of ethics.

The areas in which I have articulated personal values are integrity, congruence, love, respect, trust and loyalty, commitment, excellence, learning, communication, fun and joy, and physical fitness. Integrity underpins all my values with the first five supporting the value I place on relationships in my life, and the remainder supporting my values in relation to action focus. Each value has a quite specific definition of a sentence or two.

Short written statements on areas of behaviour that are personally important to you will define a clear base for governing your actions as you achieve your goals. They are personal standards of behaviour to which you aspire.

Set high standards and do the very best that you can to reach these standards. Striving for excellence is always rewarding. The search for perfection is almost always boring and too often doomed to failure. It is certainly one of the great barriers to productivity. So when you do occasionally fall short of a value which is important to you, do not be hard on yourself. Know that it was the best you could have done in the circumstances. There may have been the unforeseen pressure of other commitments. Use the knowledge of this momentary shortfall to improve your performance next time. It is important that you allow yourself the freedom to be human, and that you look forward to improving your performance at the next opportunity.

Show that you follow your values as closely as you can, in a really positive way. Share them with your colleagues and ask them to reflect on your performance in relation to them. This need not be time consuming and could well be part of your regular contact with them. Doing this creates a powerful bonding effect on a team or organisational environment. When your colleagues have a clear understanding of what your personal values are, and they know that your actions reflect those values, they will know precisely where they stand in their relationship with you. This level of disclosure to people with whom you have regular contact is a wonderful form of base-line communication.

You may ask why you should share values of a personal nature, such as attitudes to love and friendship, with your business colleagues. To begin with, there are no 'shoulds' about this aspect of your work. Complete openness engenders the kind of relationship that creates results. Openness is the basis of an invaluable commodity called trust, and trust is rarely seen in corporate life.[7] Be really adventurous—try sharing your values with your customers!

For me, 'love' in a business context refers to respect for the dignity of others.[8] When the people I work with know this is a fundamental tenet of my belief system, particularly if I have demonstrated that I really own this value, communication and understanding are enhanced immeasurably.

Many things in life are important; nothing need be serious! 'Joy' or 'happiness' are equally important in working relationships. Experiencing these values at work indicates you are clearly 'on purpose'. Joyful enthusiasm and commitment about what you do is based on knowing that what you do is done in the context of your values. Owning and articulating a set of guiding values is yet another part of the framework that assists you in achieving what you want. The importance of personal values is as valid, or more so, in your family life and in any sporting, social or service activity as any business activity in which you engage.

INVOLVING OTHERS

It is essential to involve all those people whose support and encouragement is critical to achieving your goal. Without close participation in this way, you cannot logically expect the support you would like. Indeed, it makes good sense to involve people in planning for your goals, even when those people are affected only tangentially. If you do not involve the people who are affected by the goal and the related action strategies, you may well find that your relationships with them will change. They may not be as supportive or productive as you might wish, and they may even become disaffected and leave your team or organisation.

Because of the strength of the focus you have on your goal, subtle changes will occur. You will say 'no' more frequently to those near you who assume your support based on your past behaviour patterns[9]. You will become so focused you will sometimes not be aware of 'environmental' distractions you might previously have noticed. You may not be so aware of a colleague's 'off day', or you may not follow up on aspects of your work not directly affected by the new direction you have set.

These changes occur once your vision and associated major

11

goal structures are in place. Communication about your vision and goals structure with people affected by them is therefore essential. It avoids misunderstandings with colleagues and does much to increase their strong contribution to your goals. The kind of involvement I suggest has almost no limits. Discuss openly and honestly with your colleagues what it means to them—do they think it important and why? Have them discuss what effect the proposed new direction will have on them, and what accommodation is necessary to harmonise your new direction with them and their own aims and ambitions.

Some form of discretion may be necessary. You may not wish, for example, to disclose your goal to succeed the company president to a close colleague who is a potential competitor for the same position. My advice is to err on the side of openness rather than discretion. I have seen too many good opportunities forfeited, or their potential diminished, simply by people's fear of being open and honest with colleagues. The risk of being 'too open' is grossly exaggerated.

PERSONAL GOALS—BALANCE

The single most significant portion of our waking hours is directly and indirectly related to our work. This is the most likely place for most of us to find an established goal structure. This might simply be budgeted sales targets or it might extend to an elaborate hierarchical set of goals based on a strong corporate vision. Whatever the nature of the corporate goals, the strength of our commitment to our work means that career and business goals predominate, if only because of basic issues of security and prestige. There is also a strong, perhaps unspoken commitment to our colleagues and any relevant professional or industry relationships essential to our work.

When your focus on work is so strong, other important aspects of your life are likely to be neglected: family, health, recreational, social, spiritual, educational and financial issues. They can all diminish when focus is strongly directed towards work. Therefore a goal structure in these areas is important. This is not to suggest that it is necessary to write a long list of major goals in each of these areas. It is sensible, however, to include each area of direct relevance to you in your overall goal structure.

In my consulting work I have met a number of senior executives who have had little or no family life as a result of their

Possible areas of interest/activity for a balanced life

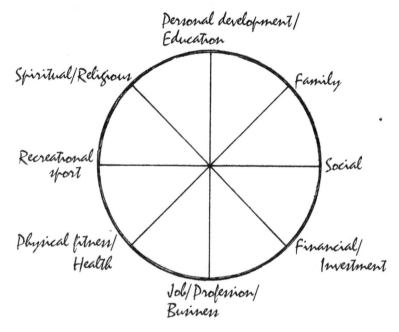

devotion to their work. Some have lost meaningful contact with their family through divorce or separation. Almost all valued their family life and were devastated by the loss. Most were completely unaware of the collapse of their family. They claimed that their commitment to their work was supporting the family by providing financial security for it.

All these people required was a shared goal about the quality of the family relationship, open communication about the demands of work, and mutual support within the family partnership for each other's goals.

In one of my seminars I was talking in this vein when a woman in her mid-thirties, married for three years with an eighteen-month old son, spoke of the business she had just begun. The success of her business was so important to her that she was prepared to sacrifice her family for it if the question ever arose. It was not that she did not care for her husband and son; she cared more for her commercial success and understood quite clearly that the potential cost of that success was acceptable to her. Had she not been so clear about her priorities, where the

13

'balance' in her life lay, she may well have ended up with her attention divided between her business and her family, making a poor job of each. I know that all of us in the seminar, including the woman herself, hoped and believed that she would not have to make the choice.

It is important here not to judge this woman's priorities by what we might understand as 'normal' community standards. She has as much right to her priorities as you have to yours. The point is to be clear about what those priorities are.

Many of us fail to address 'balance' in our lives and often lose something precious by default. For example, few of us would say that our health is unimportant to us. And yet, without conscious attention to this area of our lives, we are likely to find, too late perhaps, that our health has suffered simply because we are out of balance in our conscious and subconscious goal structure. Similarly, personal investment for retirement is often neglected by executives who are busy ensuring the long-term financial strength of their organisation.

To maintain a useful balance, identify those aspects of your life outside work that are important. Then you can assess whether the results you are experiencing are satisfactory. If not, decide what you need to do to create the results you want. Write down a goal with an associated action plan. Do this in consultation with anyone closely affected by the new direction you have set. Once this has been done arrange to review the results in six or twelve months. Decide what adjustment to make to your goal or introduce an additional goal. Write it down and plan its implementation. Assess whether there are any other areas of importance to you and where results can be enhanced.

Remember, it is not necessary to have a long list of goals in other areas. One or two goals may be enough to redress an imbalance. They are so powerful, a small amount of properly directed conscious activity can have a major impact and move you quite creatively towards full balance.

Several years ago I discovered that I had allowed my relationships with my two adult sons to deteriorate. My relationship with them had no real depth as I had allowed the level of real communication between us to diminish. My goal became to re-create my relationship with them. I wrote down an objective to the effect that at least once a month I would have dinner with them at a restaurant. Next I told them of my goal and gained their agreement to it and on a procedure to make it all happen. At first we followed the procedure carefully; now it is much more casual.

The results have been excellent. At first communication between us was stilted and forced. Now the quality of the communication between me and my children has improved wonderfully. As a bonus, I have noticed the level of communication between them has also improved. There is less aggression, more real contact and a growing friendship and respect. In effect, the reward for me is far in excess of the effort I put into creating it. And all from one quite simple goal.

PERSONAL GOALS—STRUCTURE

Simply writing down the goal is one thing, giving it a specific structure is another, although it is worthwhile noting that not all your 'goals' or 'objectives' will be spelt out in a detailed goal structure, just the most important ones. In adopting a goal structure, it is important to use one that works for you. Some people like a lot of detail in the structure, others prefer to make it as simple and as straightforward as possible. The structure that follows is merely a suggestion. The important thing is for you to decide on a structure that works for you.

The structure I like is a simple one suggested by Zig Ziglar. In one of his audio tapes he outlines a process that he claims is *essential* in ensuring that goals are achieved on schedule. A structure such as the one he advocates distinguishes between actual 'achievement' and the 'dreaming' or 'hoping' that many of us substitute for serious planning for success.[10]

1 First it is necessary to be clear about your objective.
2 Set a date for completion.
3 Identify obstacles you need to overcome in order to achieve your goal.
4 Identify the people, groups or organisations whose support you want to enlist in order to progress towards your objective.
5 Identify what you need to know to achieve your goal.
6 Set out a plan of action in order to achieve the objective.
7 Write down what you gain from its achievement. What's in it for you? Why do you want to achieve it?

You might also identify the risks in achieving your objective. Ask yourself 'What must I sacrifice to achieve my goal? What do I have to give up?'[11]. This may seem to be unduly time consuming. Remember, however, that this is what the top performers do.

In many different contexts I have noticed reference to SMART goals. This involves a goal structure meeting the following criteria:

Specific
Measurable
Agreed
Realistic
Time-bound

Specific indicates the need for precision in defining the outcome you desire. *Measurable* implies some form of measure so that you know when you have achieved your goal. *Agreed* involves the necessary congruence and agreement between what you want and those most affected by it. *Realistic* ensures that the goal stretches you beyond your present circumstances without taking you so far beyond your imagination that it is meaningless. *Time-bound* provides a time framework for the achievement of the goal.

ACTION STEPS

Once a goal has been identified, write out a strategy for implementation. Setting out your action plan, writing down the action steps required to make the goal happen and translating this into a daily commitment is your guarantee of success![12]

For each of your goals and objectives develop a number of particular action steps. The bigger and more complex the goal, the more value there is in including a detailed definition of your action steps. For example:

- things that you need to do
- people and events to follow up on
- research to accomplish
- contacts to make
- finance to arrange
- plans to develop

All action steps need to be properly articulated and itemised. Once this is done it is advisable to assign each step a time for action and a time for completion.

Writing down the action plan is the most critical step. Without a commitment to action at a more or less precise time and place, you leave it all to chance. Bringing it into conscious focus by making sure that it is done on a particular date is the most important step in the entire process. It is the one thing that makes the difference between success and failure, between a vision realised and a dream.

How you do this depends on what system works best for you. In my case I have found that the correct use of a diary 'makes things happen' for me. I am sure that pocket organisers are equally effective, as are the office automation tools of the various computer systems.

WHY WE RESIST GOAL SETTING

In the preceding paragraphs I have emphasised the power of goal setting, of the motivational value of knowing what is important to you. Yet the Harvard study mentioned earlier shows that only 3 per cent of the people surveyed had a strong formal goal structure in the manner I have described. There are a number of reasons why so few people do this. The first is the claim that there is an absence of resources with which to achieve a goal. I have often heard people in my seminars say that there is no point in writing down goals because 'I haven't enough money'—or skill or support or friends or whatever.

My response is that the reverse is the case. It is not possible to know what resources you need until you have a clear purpose in mind! I have heard many stories of people who were so committed to a goal that the necessary resources were quickly identified and obtained, even though previously they had no idea of the requirements of their goal. Sometimes this resource gathering requires conscious effort. Sometimes resources appear as if by magic. You may relate this to when you bought your first car. Everywhere you looked after you made your decision, you saw cars of the same make, model and colour. They were clearly there before. It's just that as your internal focus became clearer, your external sight began to relate to the internal focus. Things previously 'invisible' to you became visible.

I recall that when I first set up my consultancy business I had a clear need for a resource called 'clients'. Prior to writing down my goal I had no idea where I might obtain them. Indeed it was the absence of this particular resource that delayed the start of my consultancy business. As soon as I wrote down a detailed goal structure, clients seemed to materialise from nowhere. A casual meeting with a former colleague triggered an idea for possible follow-up. Talking about my plans to a friend or business contact generated further leads. In a very short period of time my list of possible clients extended into the hundreds.

Another reason for not setting goals is the notional existence of obstacles. This too is a case of putting the cart before the horse. In dealing with the issue of obstacles it is as well to recall that a fallen log across a road does not become an obstacle until you want to travel on the road. 'Things' cannot become obstacles unless and until you have articulated a direction or goal. Thinking of them as obstacles before you have written down a goal is self-limiting and self-defeating. Set your goal, identify the obstacles and deal with them.

Yet another reason for not setting goals is fear—fear of failure and fear of success. I once worked in a senior position in an organisation that was setting up a new department of about 150 people. At an early stage, I took my close colleagues away from the organisation for half a day to develop a tentative 'plan' for the department. When I showed this to my chief executive I was warned to be cautious: 'You shouldn't set people up for disappointment or failure'. He was concerned that I was setting my people goals they might not be able to meet, that they would be demotivated by the experience. There was a fear that my people might fail.

I have heard this reflected time and time again in my seminars. All the people who attend my seminars are in senior positions in their organisations. A number have in place a business-planning process to which they contribute. Few have clearly developed personal goals. The majority offer 'fear of failure' for not doing so. 'Why should I set myself up for disappointment?' 'I would rather aim low and achieve than set goals and run the risk of not reaching them.'

Fear can best be seen as an acronym for **F**alse **E**xpectations **A**ppearing **R**eal. Fear actually tells us we are onto something worthwhile! It is the risk of letting go of what is comfortable for us, of what we are used to, that holds us back from top performance. The only way to deal with fear is to acknowledge it, live with it, and move on. Risk is a fact of life.[13]

When we are doing the things we have always done we learn little, particularly if we do them well. We become closed to new ideas and limited in our capacity to stretch ourselves to new levels of performance and achievement. When we experience fear (anxiety) it is because we are involved with something new or different. Exploring this fear, and finding the value and learning in it, is one of the most powerful things you can do to develop your full potential. Fear of success is closely related to fear of failure in the way it limits our potential. When we are comfortable, we are likely to see any change, even success, as being a threat to us, even if the threat is only subconsciously experienced.

A strong goal structure breaks through the barrier of fear and uncertainty about what the future might hold, and stretches us to higher and higher levels of performance. Setting goals is the beginning of the process of moving towards new areas of comfort. The extent to which we can visualise the completed outcomes of the goals we set ourselves *in advance of their achievement*, is the extent to which our 'comfort' stretches to include the new goals.[14]

When you are genuinely concerned about the possibility of setting your sights too high, try deciding on a range for your performance expectations. Decide at one level what you could achieve without much additional conscious effort. Decide at another what you could do if you pulled out all reasonable stops. Make this range the focus for your planning. You cannot fail to achieve your minimum position and are almost guaranteed to achieve well beyond it. Once you have become more confident, start reaching for the sky!

SUPPORTING YOUR VISION AND GOALS WITH END-RESULT IMAGERY

Achievement is also affected by the extent to which you can visualise your goal in the present tense; the intensity with which you can actually feel you possess that goal *now*. Creative visualisation is a technique that has been used by top athletes, people in the performing arts, and top achievers generally for several decades now. It is a simple process involving bringing to your mind a picture of a completed project: a gold medal and new world record with the applause of the crowd ringing in your ears; a major theatrical work completed, to strong critical acclaim; a product launch or difficult negotiation completed to your organisation's complete satisfaction, with your own part in it fully acknowledged. The literature of management studies and the psychology of human performance is full of examples of how this works, of how effective creative imagination is in bringing us to a successful conclusion in a particular career or personal goal.[15]

Some time ago I was introduced to a story about Mike Vance, a senior Disney executive. He was touring Disneyworld in Florida for the first time, accompanied by a young assistant. It was not long after Walt Disney's death and the assistant said, after viewing the magnificence of the completed construction: 'What a pity Walt didn't see this'. Vance looked at his assistant with a slightly raised eyebrow and said, 'He did!'. It was the strength of Walt Disney's vision that was the foundation of his work.

When the vision, and the major goals that serve it, are vivid in your imagination, when you can almost touch or feel the ultimate outcome, its achievement is as natural as life itself. There is almost a sense of *déjà vu* when the goal is achieved. Perhaps your own experience in managing small tasks shows you how this works. When the task is immediate, it is easy to 'see' the end result. Achievement then is a matter of course. So it is with larger lifetime goals; the process is one of articulation, then visualisation through creative imagination. When you have strong images of a completed end point in mind, the desired results are certain.

The essence of the concept is a strong visual image of the end result you want. The stronger the image you are able to create, the more likely it is that you will achieve the outcome. This is not a magic approach. Top performers are using it increasingly as they appreciate its value in driving them to the levels of performance to which they aspire. Listen to the interviews given by athletes, sports people and artists as they describe the extent of the advance preparation they do in imagery practice.

A close colleague of mine is dedicated to motor racing. He works full time as a graphic designer and communications consultant, although he has a burning desire to be a professional race driver. For longer than he cares to admit his lap times reflected a second order performance, some 1.8 seconds short of what was required to reach his goal. After I introduced him to creative visualisation, he spent 10 minutes each day for a week visualising himself in his car taking the line around the corner much tighter than he had ever been able to do in the past. The next weekend his lap time was reduced by 2.1 seconds and he was on his way to his dream.

The way visualisation seems to work is to override the restricting or limiting mental images that are produced in an anxiety state. For the vast majority of us, our minds can only focus on one thing at a time, however much it might jump from one thing to another with lightning speed. The strength of a commitment to the image of a positive end result is the extent to which the limiting patterns of thought are overridden.

Sit in a comfortable chair, feet flat on the floor, arms resting easily and uncrossed, and close your eyes. Take a number of slow deep breaths and imagine drawing air into your whole body, letting each breath out slowly, while gently relaxing the body. Imagine what the *successfully* completed task will look, feel, sound and smell like. Picture the completed task, the people concerned and see it all 'wrapped up' and delivered on time to everyone's satisfaction.

End-result imagery or creative visualisation is probably one of the most under-used processes available to us, yet it is the easiest and the most powerful tool to use for performance improvement.

CONCLUSION

Whether you are designing a personal lifetime goal, personal values, goals or objectives, it is important for you to be conscious of them, to write them down, and communicate them regularly to the people with whom you work. Apart from being a wonderful stress reducer,[16] written goals and values have an extremely powerful effect on performance.

It is important that goals and goal structures are flexible—they are a statement today of what you expect of your tomorrow. Be open to new information and changes of attitude and beliefs, and be free to change the goals and values you hold whenever appropriate. After all, the importance lies not in the actual goal or the particular value; it is in the activity that the goal and value generate. The journey has more significance than the destination.

A goal structure shows you exactly what is at risk when new information or opportunity is presented to you. Without a goal structure by which to measure the new information or opportunity, you risk allowing yourself to be governed by the crisis of the moment. A goal structure, therefore, provides the very basis of flexibility in a work environment.

A goal structure provides an organised framework for decisions and actions; it concentrates action in a liberating and productive way. Life should not be something that happens to us because we are too lazy or indecisive to grasp the wonderful opportunities we attract. Life and success are what we create for ourselves.

21

KEY MESSAGES FROM CHAPTER 1

- *Work with close friends and colleagues in deciding what your personal lifetime goals might be. Write them down on several small cards. Place one in your wallet, another in your diary, another on your desk. Consciously look at it a number of times each day. Imagine what it would be like to actually know that you had achieved your lifetime goal as you read.*

- *Write down a set of values in areas that are important to you. Show them to your family and encourage them to write down their own values. Talk about them to your work colleagues. Ask family and friends to support you in living according to your values. Make sure they are free to speak to you about them, particularly when you fall short of them in any way.*

- *Decide what key areas of your life are important to you and write down a goal or two in each major area. Decide which of them are the most important. Write out a detailed goal structure for the most important. Talk to your family, friends and work colleagues about them. Enlist their support where practicable.*

- *Select an important goal and spend 5–10 minutes each day for a fortnight or so resting with your eyes closed imagining, as strongly as you can, the goal achieved to your full satisfaction. Experience the achievement of your goal in every way possible.*

- *Develop a detailed action plan for each major goal and make commitments in your diary for the particular actions necessary to bring them to fruition.*

CHAPTER 2

Focused attention for organisational success

There is a strong relationship between personal goals, the business-planning process and the success of a particular organisation, whether it be a small private business, a large public company or some form of government organisation. A successful organisation is one in which the values and the goals and ambitions of the individuals who comprise it are in harmony with those of the organisation. This is one of the key elements of the relationship between the individual and the organisation.[1]

The relationship between personal performance and the environment in which a person operates is one of interdependence. Most of us spend the largest proportion of our waking hours at work. Our performance relates closely to how good we feel about what we do and to the environment in which we work.

This chapter is about how the business-planning and development process can be undertaken so that the relationship between the vision, values and goals of the organisation and the genuine and legitimate aspirations (goals) of the people who comprise it work to the advantage of both. It is not an exhaustive study of the subject of business planning.[2] It simply touches on a few key areas of planning for success in an organisation.

The key areas are: the need for a more elaborate structure of goals at each functional level of an organisation; the relationship between corporate, divisional and departmental goals and plans and those of teams and individuals; and the need for there to be a process whereby the contribution of the people who comprise the organisation is integral to the gaol setting and planning process.

Planning is about bringing goals to fruition. Achieving a goal through articulation of the goal alone will rarely be enough to activate larger, more complex goals. A goal that taps into the 'essence' in the people in your team or organisation has a quite distinct advantage. Goals of this nature are of the kind seen in top athletes, the stars of the entertainment world, and some business and professional people who seem to be totally consumed by their ambitions. It is seen only in organisations prepared to invest the time and energy in developing the skills of leadership throughout the organisation. To make things happen in your team, or in your organisation, it is necessary to take steps to gather the resources of facts, funds and personnel to help you achieve those goals. Planning is necessary to bring your goals to fruition. This is best undertaken by involving the people in your team and organisation in the process.

GOAL STRUCTURES FOR BUSINESS PLANNING

Establishing a useful goal structure for a business is a multifaceted exercise. Organisations can be large and complex, and the goal is likely to be correspondingly complex. The number of people involved in its implementation adds another dimension to the process.

In the course of my consulting career, I have seen a wide range of procedures used to establish goals for an organisation, and a confusing variety of names, used in an attempt to indicate the hierarchical nature of the structure. For the most part it is valid to conclude that, if it works and the results are there for you, continue with the process you have. There is some sense in the adage, 'If it ain't broke, don't fix it!', although in the rapidly changing environment that characterises the business climate of the 1990s—the one likely to be with us into the new century—there is also sense in continually looking out for innovative ways to facilitate the planning process.[3]

If you have no formal business-planning structure, or perhaps wish to review the structure you have, you may like to follow the suggestions made here. A structure for business-planning activity is hierarchical in nature with the need for increasing detail as the hierarchy descends: vision, mission and values, operating principles; major business goals; objectives; and action steps. Clearly the decision on the ultimate nature of the vision or goal rests with the team or organisational leadership. It makes sense to increase the involvement of the front-line people in the implementation of the goal as much as possible. As the process becomes more detailed the involvement naturally becomes greater.

Vision and values

A corporate vision is a simple statement of your main business purpose. It should be short and emotive, capturing the essence of what you want to create. It might include a straightforward enunciation of the major business direction of the moment, something each member of the organisation knows about and works towards: exports, cost reduction, excellence, service, etc. Corporate values are succinct statements of the values of the organisation in key areas. Again simplicity and commitment are the cornerstones of a good value statement.

Designing statements of corporate vision and values should be an exercise in which every member of your organisation has an opportunity to participate. It is rare that statements issued by a chief executive or a board of directors have any real effect although there have been a relatively small number of celebrated examples of an effective vision imposed by a strong (founding) leader: IBM, McDonalds, Disney. Generally, however, strong 'bottom-up' ownership is the way to ensure that the majority of people in the organisation understand and value the statements and are committed to them. After all, this is the purpose of the exercise. This process begins with each functional work team, whether front-line or support, deciding which values are important to its successful operation. At this point, values might be expressed in words or phrases rather than in profound detailed statements.

Each team is asked to articulate a team mission—what is their main purpose, what special role do they play in the whole. The senior management team and board of directors should also set out the values and vision they have for themselves as a team. Once this is done it is necessary for a specially selected group to sift through the views expressed throughout the organisation and settle on core values and vision. This is discussed with each team and their reactions are sought. These reactions are incorporated into the 'final' statements agreed on by the board of directors. It is wise for an organisation to maintain, within reason, a continual process of review, so that the relevance of its statement of vision and value is maintained. This way a statement of vision and values remains fluid.

I have seen some very succinct statements of vision and values, and I have also seen many more longer, elaborate statements. I have seen many that have been issued by the board of directors with the advice of the senior management. I have seen a few that have been genuinely derived from a consultative process. However they are expressed, it is important that they represent the essential purpose and the common values of the people and the organisation. It is also essential that everyone in the organisation knows what the statement means and what they must do to give it life in their own area of expertise.

Once the vision is in place, it is the role of the senior executive team and of team leaders generally to ensure that the vision remains visible and relevant to the organisation. Test major decisions against the vision and values. Make sure that they appear in annual reports and prospectuses. Arrange for them to be displayed in the premises of the organisation—in public places, and in all the places where people meet and work. Have coffee mugs made with the vision clearly printed on them. Issue them to everyone or hand them out as prizes for performance.

Operating principles

A statement of operating principles is a carefully designed articulation of the boundaries of responsibility, within which the people in the team within an organisation may act in order to achieve their goals and objectives. The principles may apply across the entire organisation or just to a specific team. Goals and objectives are statements of outcomes or results you want to achieve. They are not statements of process or method.

People, both individually and in teams, work best when they are able to achieve their results without being too obviously restricted in the process. This is an important aspect of motivation. There is a compelling inner need in most of us for freedom to do things our own way. There is a parallel need for direction and guidelines. Too much freedom and the uncertainty of being able to relate performance to a notional benchmark is highly demotivating. If there is too much restriction placed on initiative, enthusiasm for the task is reduced, with a consequent lowering of motivation. The challenge for leaders of teams of people is to provide the appropriate balance.

Operating principles may also include an additional or

extended capacity to act in emergency situations. Here, an example might be that the team responsible for the data-processing facility has a freedom to spend three times their normal limit under specifically defined conditions such as a facility failure of certain prescribed dimensions, in order to maintain customer service expectations.

Operating principles might also be general statements of policy in relation to customer service, supplier relationships, the relationships of the people within the organisation or financial accountability. They might be generally applicable to all people in the organisation or quite specific in their reference to financial delegation, travel arrangements or purchasing procedures. They might be specific to particular functions or activities. For example, a task force charged with introducing a new warehousing system might be given an upper limit of total expenditure and a range of parameters on location, access or relationship to major freight terminals and customs facilities; beyond these broad parameters they are free to act for the entire organisation.

Using relevant and appropriate operating principles, the message is—once the major business goals and objectives are drawn up—your team is free to act, providing they do so within the operating principles. They must seek approval if they want to act outside them.

Accountability standards and procedures may also be articulated in the context of operating principles.

The key is for there to be as few constraints as possible coupled with widespread understanding and application. Apply closer guidelines for more particular work teams and for special application whenever necessary. Remember, too close a reign on personal initiative is as demotivating as too little, and what works well for one team may not work so well for another. The way to design operating principles that provide this essential balance is to ask the people involved. Seek individual and team input. Ask them what they need to carry out their task. If they request too much freedom, sit down with them and discuss accountability and work out a compromise that suits both of you. If they seem to be showing too little initiative, work with them in finding out why, and find a way for them to extend themselves.

When properly designed, with the right balance between initiative and constraint, operating principles are a powerful way of making sure that a task is performed at a high level. This ensures that those involved are extending their performance at every opportunity. The result is happy and committed people in your team.

Business goals

Major business goals are statements of the major outcomes required for meeting the organisation's vision. They might be expressed in market share, turnover of product or product range, safety standards, profitability by cost centre or staff and customer satisfaction.

Major business goals should be carefully designed to be congruent with the vision.[4] Ideally there will be two or three major statements of this kind for each separate business activity. For a work team within an organisation there might be just one. For example, a team charged with the development of a new market strategy for a product range might be given a quite specific business goal expressed in market share, image, profitability and so on.

Objectives and specific action steps

Objectives are specific statements of expected achievements or outcomes that will give effect to the major business goals. They are the 'engine room' of the planning process. Even at the corporate level, they are sufficiently specific to base goal setting and planning at lower levels of the corporate structure. There might well be ten or twenty statements of objectives to support each major goal. Being specific is very important; a properly designed set of objectives would answer the following questions:

- What precisely is to be achieved?
- Who is responsible for making it happen?
- When is it to be completed?
- To what particular performance standards?
- What test of satisfactory completion will there be?

When objectives fit nicely with the major business goals and the vision, they provide significant motivation for the majority of the people in the organisation. They underline the need for precision in defining the expected outcomes contained in the major business goals.

Objectives should always be quantifiable.

Both objectives and specific action steps are elements of the goal structure of an organisation and are best left to the teams

28

responsible for them. Your role as leader is to work with them in articulating the larger outcomes required, to see that they have an effective set of objectives and action steps in place. Their role is to get on with the job within the parameters set by the operating principles of the team or organisation. Your people will be much more motivated if they have a direct, almost exclusive, role to play in devising the implementation phase of the process.

Specific action steps are statements of the actions necessary to bring about the results spelt out in your objectives. Action steps should be designed by the people who are directly responsible for those results. For each objective, the action steps might be singular or many and varied. They should specify the person or team responsible for their completion. They should also be quite specific about the time of anticipated completion. Beyond this, action steps are sometimes qualitative and sometimes quantitative. The degree to which they are quantifiable depends on the nature of the objective they serve.

This section discusses in greater detail the nature of the business objective and the need for it to be measurable and tangible.

WRITING BUSINESS OBJECTIVES

Vision is the context in which the goals and objectives of an organisation are set. It is the overall motivating force behind an organisation. The combination of the 'goal' and 'objective' and 'specific action steps' is the basis of results the organisation achieves.

The golden rule of business objectives is that they have little value if they are not specific and measurable. General or intangible objectives may sometimes have an effect; they are certainly better than not having any. When they are expressed in specific and measurable form, their power is considerably increased. If being the 'best widget maker in town' is important to you, translate what you mean by 'best' into some quantifiable form. Performance criteria of an objective nature should be attached to the objective. For example, there is significantly more point to 'being the largest widget maker by turnover and by gross profit'. Similarly, there is less point to an objective to 'sell more widgets' than to one which requires you to 'sell 10 per cent more widgets in the fourth quarter of this year than in the corresponding quarter of the previous year'.

Specific objectives form a much stronger basis for follow-up procedures and acknowledgement after achievement. Specific goals allow you to identify under-achievement and to introduce appropriate remedial action: 'Lift production of widgets by 15 per cent', 'Cut costs of production of widgets by 5 per cent', 'Reduce accident rates on the widget production line by 15 per cent'. Properly associated with an appropriate time frame, these are powerful objectives with a creative and positive effect on performance. Reduction of inventory levels, of the incidence of shop-lifting and of absenteeism are all targets you can quantify quite readily.

There is value in you and your staff being able to see and feel the objective, to plan for its achievement, and to see progress towards it. Bringing the objective into specific measurable focus enables you to take whatever corrective action may be necessary and to know that you have been effective. A seemingly non-quantifiable goal can, with thought, almost always be given some numeric expression. Customer satisfaction or employee morale, for example, can be surveyed and the results used to indicate remedial action. They also provide a basis of comparison with future surveys.

A word of caution: when converting subjectively framed objectives to a notional numeric form, always treat the resulting 'measurement' with sufficient flexibility to maintain the confidence of all participants in the goal structure. Flexibility is, after all, a key element in all effective management. For example, it is important to remain aware that the 'numbers' represent a value judgement, particularly when reviewing performance. As such, they are not an end in themselves and should always be used in that context. Referring back to the values that underlie the numbers may sometimes be warranted. Another important point to remember is that objectives that are patently not achievable, given the resources reasonably available to your organisation, are counter-productive. There is little point in setting an objective that is out of reach for you or your colleagues. Performance improvement is essentially a function of the people involved. There is a nice balance to be reached between stretching them to improve their performance by means of well-designed objectives and demotivating them if the objectives are patently absurd.

Goals, on the other hand, may be less tangible in form. The 'impossible dream' is always achievable provided you and your team are prepared to put sufficient energy into it. Set a realistic time frame for achievement and carefully plan the steps towards the 'dream'. Plan also for the acquisition of the resources you need—knowledge, materials, finance and skills. Communicate your goal and the plans you have for achieving it to all those people who are to be involved; they will need to be as convinced of its ultimate practicability as you are.

Do not exclude goals that initially seem impossible to reach. A structure of objectives can always be carefully designed to contribute positively to an overall goal, however fanciful the goal may seem at first.

A PLANNING HIERARCHY

Business planning is distinct from personal goal setting, in that it is much more likely to have a hierarchical structure of the kind set out in the preceding paragraphs. The number of stages in the planning process will depend on the size of the organisation. For large multifaceted organisations there may be many tiers. In smaller organisations the business plan may look more like a personal goal structure.

A large organisation will have an overall corporate plan. Each of the organisation's divisions—whether geographic or product based—will have its own plan, as will each department of each division. Similarly, work teams and individuals within teams will have their own business plans. The individual business plan may be incorporated into position descriptions and form part of a performance expectation agreement scheme.

In most organisations, you will notice that the formal corporate plan exists as a glossy formal document, often prepared at considerable expense. It may well have its counterpart at divisional or even departmental level. It is almost always less clearly defined for the team and the individual. When you consider that this is where the product line is, where the real point of client service contact is, where the delivery of corporate objectives ultimately happens, you begin to wonder at the value of the planning undertaken. This is almost always because the front-line people of the organisation have not been closely involved in the planning process. When this involvement does occur, team and individual objectives and their performance expectations become clearer.

This close involvement creates both momentum in an organisation and motivation for the people within it.

31

INVOLVEMENT

When the aims and ambitions of the people of an organisation closely relate to the vision, values and business direction of their organisation, the organisation is effective and dynamic. Work is a good place to be, staff relationships are good, customer service is excellent and productivity is high. Creating a clear set of objectives for work teams and for individuals is essentially an exercise for the team and its people. It is part of good team leadership to involve your team in the design, measurement and rewards of the structure of objectives for the team.

Impose objectives as a unilateral exercise and the choices you have in maintaining high levels of performance are limited. If you do not take strong action, you are at risk of being seen as an ineffective leader. On the other hand, if you involve your people closely in setting their own and the team objectives, you have created a positive commitment to success in them. This provides a wider choice for you as team leader in coaching and supporting your people towards achievement.

The essential components of a highly focused, motivated and productive organisation or team of people are:

- specific action steps taken by individuals within an organisation or a team must be aligned with their set of operational objectives;
- the operational objectives should, in turn, be aligned with the major business goals; and
- the business goals should be aligned with the vision of the organisation.

When there is a strong correlation between the actions individuals take on the shop floor, or at the customer interface, and the vision and values of the organisation, the climate for motivation and commitment is at its optimum.

A 'top down' planning process is generally regarded with cynicism at the working level of the organisation. Creating a 'bottom up' planning process through positive involvement will create a strong relationship between what teams and individuals actually do and the corporate plan. Bottom up visioning and planning is time consuming and often difficult, although the long-term rewards of such an open process have always been obvious for those with the personal commitment to work in this way.

As organisations become more and more complex, the tendency is to impose more and more control. A wise man once told me that the only way to truly be 'in control' was to give up control. By this he meant that if you have done your job well in setting up the basic parameters of performance expectation within clear operating principles, everything will fall into place. He had, in effect, assumed total control by sharing control and so avoiding the more rigid control models of the past. Monitoring and control relate to the specific nature of the task, and to the skills and motivation of the individual undertaking the task, rather than to a resource-hungry monolith.[5]

When team leaders involve their people in this way, there is a degree of ownership at the front-line that means the team leaders have to spend much less time monitoring and controlling the activities of their teams. They are free to spend more time doing those things that being a leader is all about: getting to know the staff, concentrating on other internal and external public profile activities, team building, and building new ventures and approaches into the corporate structure.

Inspire your people at a grassroots level and set them free to perform within your organisation's operating principles, values and vision.

Ownership and commitment are great motivating forces. Create a positive expectation of your people's commitment and involve them in setting their performance standards and your major business goals will be achieved.

CREATING RESULTS FROM YOUR BUSINESS PLAN

Once you have created a business-planning structure including vision, values, major business goals, objectives and specific action steps, it is necessary to decide on the people who will bring the specific action steps to the results you want and by what deadlines. This provides a basis for review and reappraisal of the people who will execute the plan.

In putting the final touches to the business plan I have always found it useful to ask individuals and teams for their own schedule of completion expectation. If the response differs substantially from corporate expectations, a useful discussion about priorities and performance efficiency can ensue. The value lies in the way the process builds commitment in the people who are responsible for the action. You are entitled to have much more confidence in the agreed plan as a result.

When giving greater responsibility to your people in deciding the detail of the plan, be aware of their propensity to over-commit. Your role as leader is to ensure your colleagues are stretched and not demotivated by so large a number of tasks that they have little hope of achieving them all.

When you and your team are creating a detailed set of action steps to bring a goal or objective to fruition, you might consider looking at a process I call 'multidimensional planning'. This is extremely valuable in all circumstances, and is particularly useful in breaking down the more complex tasks into action steps.

A MULTIDIMENSIONAL APPROACH TO PLANNING

The technique I use follows the 'mind-mapping' technique described by Tony Buzan in his books on integrating the creative or right side of the brain with the (normally dominant) analytical left side.[6] There is an example of a mind map set out on the following page. It is a very particular form of brainstorming.

The most important element of any brainstorming exercise is that there be no hierarchy in the group you have gathered for the purpose. Hierarchy sits uneasily in the modern work team; it has no place in a brainstorming session. The object is to get as many *ideas* out into the open as possible without judging them. Make it clear that there is, for the time being, no such thing as an irrational or ill-conceived idea or thought. At a later stage, judgements can be made on the relevance, cost or practicability of the ideas generated; this is not part of the brainstorming function.

Team brainstorming using the mind-mapping technique is a very useful way to ensure maximum creative input. It is most effective when the ideas are expressed graphically rather than in linear fashion. This is the advantage of the mind-mapping process. You begin by identifying your project name or objective in the centre of a single piece of paper. Working in the traditional way on a flipboard with butcher's paper is most effective. An electronic whiteboard is also useful as it provides an opportunity to copy the results of your work to all team members for further action.

Based on the ideas generated by your group, you set out in radial lines, much like a spider web, the key elements of your

The key elements of this chapter expressed as a mind map

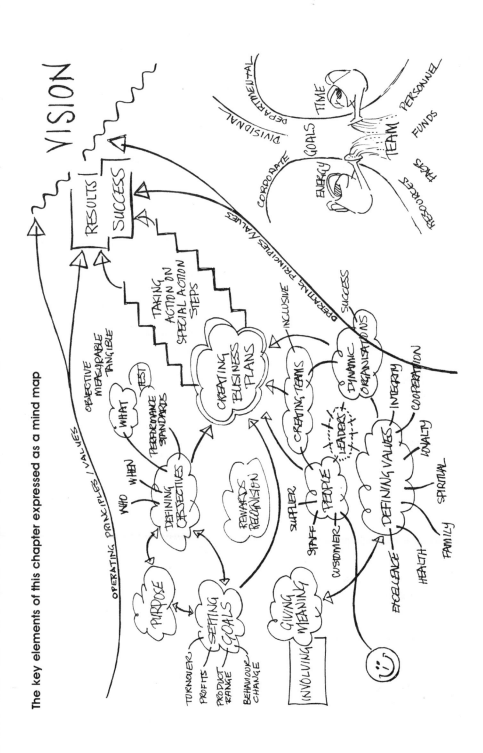

project. Radiating from each of these lines will be further lines identifying the sub-elements. This gives a graphic and therefore obvious representation of any areas of overlap, interdependency and interrelationship.

The 'messy' nature of the exercise is one of its greatest values. It should be fun, indeed riotously so; the more fun the better, as the 'fun' element of the exercise is the very basis of its creativity. Out of the silliest idea or concept might come the germ of a more practical and effective way of achieving your outcome. To close down on such creativity is to limit the possibility of innovative creative responses to complex tasks. Probably much more importantly, it closes down on the degree of participation and involvement; ownership by the members of the team is reduced.

A single element or arm of your spider web may be sufficiently complex in its own right as to make it sensible for you devote a separate mind-mapping session to it.

Once the mind maps are complete you need to re-draw your 'spider' or mind map of the task ahead, cleaning it up in the process. Then, and only then, is it time to examine the number of alternative action possibilities you have identified. Examine them all, discount some and modify others. Ultimately you will have a final version of 'the plan' which takes account of all the appropriate interdependencies and relationships in a way that was hidden from you in straightforward linear or time-sequential planning. Often writing down a 'plan' in a time-sequential way locks you into a fixed relationship between one element of the plan and another. Mind mapping lets you quickly review the overall task in a holistic way. This in turn permits a flexible response to the task.

Once the mind map has been completed and the decisions made, extract discrete action elements from it and translate them into time-sequential form. Milestones, dependencies, delegations and responsibilities may now be written into diaries or other forms of action schedules.[7] Follow-up dates and major reviews of progress should also be identified and recorded to help you monitor progress.

CONCLUSION

I liken the alignment of the business vision and plans of a business with the aims and ambitions of the individuals who comprise the business to the way a magnet works. A piece of iron or steel acts as a magnet when the molecules of the steel are aligned in the same direction. Without this alignment of molecules the piece of metal is dead and reactive to outside forces only. Once the molecules are aligned it becomes a powerful force in its own right. So it is when an organisation makes the effort to involve its people in designing its vision, values and major goals.

This is an important and vital challenge for leaders: building teams of people who are able to express and serve their own objectives within the vision and objectives of the organisation.

KEY MESSAGES FROM CHAPTER 2

- *Design a vision and value statement for your team. Involve your entire team in doing this. Have the resulting statements form a continuing part of your team relationships in as many ways as you and your team can devise.*

- *Establish operating principles by which you and your team are able to work without detailed and continuous reference to your organisation's management.*

- *Write down the business goals or statements of major outcomes that will contribute to you achieving your corporate vision and values.*

- *Make sure your major team objectives are precisely spelt out so that you know what is to be achieved, by whom, by when, and to what particular performance standards. Know what test there will be of satisfactory completion.*

- *Involve your team in all the decisions relating to the design of specific objectives and the action steps that will bring them to fruition.*

- *Use the 'mind-mapping' technique to tease out ideas and actions necessary for the implementation of your team objectives. Use it to cross-reference team activity, and to increase teamwork. Use it also to solve some of the team's more difficult problems.*

CHAPTER 3

Staying on track 1

Now that you have a strong focus on what is important for you and on what you want to achieve, it is time to look at some of the ways to maintain focus on a day-to-day basis.

In the previous chapter I said that once a goal is written down and you have set out the relevant action steps necessary to bring the goal to a successful outcome, the energy of the goal creates its own momentum. This is true in every instance.

When you are busy and productive, you have a larger number of goals and responsibilities than if you are more narrowly focused. The way you work—whether you work in a highly structured environment or whether you work for yourself—will largely determine the level of personal support you have available for maintaining your focus on your principal goals. The principles of how you maintain focus are substantially the same.

The essential point is that you maintain your focus to create the outcomes you want. If you do not, you permit distraction and risk poor performance. This chapter looks at some basic principles of human behaviour which you can use for maintaining focus. Not all the principles will apply equally. This discussion of the principles here is merely designed to raise your awareness of how you spend your time. It will suggest ways of looking at your work and prompt a much more effective use of your productive capacity.

LEVERAGE

Leverage activity is activity that produces results greater than the amount of effort put into achieving the result. A block and tackle is an ideal example of leverage at work. Using a block and tackle, you can lift weights that are considerably heavier than you would otherwise be able to lift. The actual weight you can lift depends on the gearing of the block and tackle. The amount of energy you must exert is disproportionate to the physical weight of the object you can lift with the block and tackle.

Another example is the use of the merge facility on a word processor in order to customiśe letters or mail-outs to clients. If this technology were not available, you would have to custom type individual letters or adopt a very impersonal approach through a circular letter. The first method is very expensive, in both time and money, and the second is ineffective by virtue of its impersonal approach.

Proper use of a secretary or personal assistant is another example of leveraging your time effectively. Full communication and involvement is the key to devolving far more responsibility upon our personal assistants than currently seems possible. It is your responsibility as team leader to spend as much time as possible on highly productive activities which require your direct attention.

Maturity in management and leadership depends on the ability to spend time on high leverage activity naturally and spontaneously, without a crisis forcing you to do so. Indeed, if you do not spend adequate time on high leverage activity, you can fully expect to spend much more of your time being over-committed, giving inadequate amounts of time and attention to one crisis after another.

There are a number of generic categories of high leverage activity: goal setting and planning, organising, training, communication and feedback.

Goal setting and planning

The need for creating an effective definition of focus through conscious goal setting and planning is a constant theme of this book. It is worth mentioning that the time you spend on defining your focus has extraordinary value. It is essential that you focus on high leverage activity in personal and business activities. It is all too easy to overlook, or put off, goal setting and planning activity as we react to the demands of the moment: client calls, staff matters and meetings often distract us from setting and maintaining focus.

The key here is the word 'react'. When you react to circumstances as a way of life you become over-committed and 'out of control'. With proper attention to focus through goal setting and planning, you are much more likely to be able to set your own agenda and become much less reactive to events. This does not mean single-minded dedication to tasks while being oblivious to the personal needs of your customers, staff and colleagues. If you are able to focus clearly on your main purpose *when it is appropriate to do so*, you are able to deal with clients, staff and colleagues without resentment and far more effectively.

Organising

Time spent on this aspect of your work is high leverage work also. 'Organising' may relate to personal office procedures, relationships between you and your personal staff, appropriate delegation with follow-up and feedback procedures properly in place, structural review, work practice analysis, automating key functions or introducing technological improvements.

It is important that the 'organising' is appropriate and relevant. (In the course of my working and consulting career I have seen 'busy' executives spending a lot of energy 'organising' and 'reorganising' to the point where they were not very productive at all. This is akin to rearranging the deck chairs on the *Titanic*. Organising may relate to simple matters such as restructuring your office to reduce the chance of interruptions, or spending more time on complex administrative change. Whatever its form, well-directed organising is high leverage activity.

Work practice analysis is one particular form of organising activity that is of considerable value. Conducted by small teams of people, who are representative of all people in your organisation and who are affected by the particular practice, including people from teams other than your own, this analysis provides the basis of considerable productivity improvement. Minor suggestions for improvements and redesign of procedures that are outdated or otherwise hinder more productive activity are certain to be implemented if they are drawn from those most affected by them.

A continual process of work practice analysis is the hallmark of highly effective organisations. Encourage it in your team

40

as much as possible. It is of great ongoing value to develop a 'best practices' statement for key tasks in your team by encouraging looking outside your team and organisation at alternative methods.

Structural review is only useful when the structure is substantially out of line with the organisation's purpose and direction. In general, structure is far less important than the informal relationships that make up the real 'structure' of an organisation. Tinkering with structure rarely means anything to the people who are directly responsible for the team's results.

Organising at a personal level is covered in a substantive way elsewhere in this book. See in particular Chapter 10, 'Action planning—organising your day', and Chapter 11, 'Using your diary'.

Training

Training is another form of high leverage activity. This applies to technical or professional training and personal development training. Training is high leverage activity in the sense that the time spent in learning new skills and new understandings about the way people work together produces an ongoing improvement in productivity that is significantly greater than the cost in time and money of the training program itself.

Training is an activity which should be strictly tailored to the needs of individuals *in the context of properly designed goals and priorities*. I have seen organisations spend substantial amounts of time and money on training that has been largely dictated by the personal whims of staff. This is due to the absence of a coordinated staff development strategy, designed to relate closely to the goals and objectives of the organisation and of the people who comprise it.

It is important that any commitment to training is consistent with the ability of the organisation or team to maintain satisfactory levels of production or service. It is not good enough to place a sign on a branch office window or leave a recorded message on your phone system to the effect that your office is closed in order to provide training for your staff. Staggered hours and after-hours attendance at training programs are an obvious alternative that will appeal to committed people.

Training needs should be properly assessed and the training provided should be closely related to the goals and objectives of the organisation and to the developmental needs of the people in it.

Once you have decided on the training program, the message you give to each person attending is critical to the value you, and the person concerned, receives from it. This means counselling each participant before and after a training program. Ideally a person attends a training program because it is something you have jointly identified as being useful or necessary to their development in their job. It is your responsibility to make it perfectly clear to your colleague why they are attending. You will want to discuss with them your expectations of their attendance and find out what their expectations might be. You will want to relate this to the personal objectives of your colleague and to the objectives of your team.

After the training program has been completed, it is important to discuss what value they obtained from the training, to discover whether your expectations and those of your staff were met. You might inquire whether they have any suggestions for its improvement and how the skills or understandings learnt can be extended to other staff. Also important is discovering how you can support your staff in applying those skills and understandings.

If the training is internally resourced, evaluation information will give you valuable feedback for subsequent course development. If the course is external, the evaluation will enable you to assess the usefulness in sending other staff to the same course and any other courses conducted by that provider.

Ideally the training program will derive from an appraisal system, designed to match the career development of the individual with the goals of the organisation. Many organisations I have experienced undertake some form of training needs analysis. Very few have a training program integrated with an individual development program *in an effective way*. None include *ante* and *post hoc* counselling as routine procedures.

It is much easier for many managers to justify 'skills' or technical and professional training than personal development training. If a member of your staff has a particular skill deficiency, is otherwise well regarded and there is a course available appropriate to the need, the training is readily justified. Results from training in personal development areas are much less tangible. Time management, team building, communication and the skills of human interrelationships and leadership are all important. Because of the importance of the need for these 'soft' skills, it is important that courses are selected with care and that evaluation counselling be quite thorough.

Time spent on properly designing a training profile for you and your staff is high leverage activity. So too is the time spent on attending a training course as part of that program.

Communication

Communication and feedback are the most critical forms of high leverage activity. Because good communication and feedback necessarily involve openness and honesty of purpose, they tend to be areas in which we are less comfortable and, therefore, use less well. When we have to tell a colleague something that we fear might be embarrassing or offensive, there is a tendency to creatively avoid fully communicating with them. It is sad that this is so, for it is only out of complete and honest communication that real understanding and the best of working relationships develop.

Communication is the one activity we need most when we are at our busiest. Ironically, that is the time when we engage in it least.

However clear the result you want is to you, a failure to communicate with your people will put the basis of a proper working relationship with them at risk. Some of the more common omissions include:

- giving a full and complete definition of a new task or project;
- providing the full context of a particular task;
- providing a completion time or indicating a standard of completion;
- indicating the amount of time that should be spent on a task;
- properly articulating relevant operating principles or the limits of financial or human resources for the task; and
- properly communicating milestones for review or other ongoing feedback requirements.

If any one of these aspects of communication is missing, there is an increased risk of something going wrong. When your communication is incomplete, your unspoken expectation can hardly be met, except perhaps by coincidence. Incomplete communication results in misunderstandings which are always counter-productive. You spend time correcting the mistake, and re-establishing the full communication, and you have to pacify a colleague, or

43

worse, an upset customer. You are diverted from other more productive activity.

Complete communication is vital in establishing and maintaining good relationships with customers, work colleagues, professional colleagues and other people with whom you relate in business. It is also a most valuable asset in establishing and maintaining good family relationships. If communication is so important, pay attention to it, particularly when you are busy.

Communication styles

When communicating with people, have some idea of the dominant communication style of the person with whom you are dealing and their underlying needs. The chart on page 45 indicates one way of understanding the differences that exist between people in the way they communicate.

Passive/task-oriented people look for detail in communication; they are the analytical types. Their basic need is for accuracy and perfection. Assertive/task-oriented people want direction and have a strong need to get things done. They will not react well to long, involved instructions particularly about *how* to do something. They need to be in control.

Passive/people types thrive on warm close relationships. They need approval. They need a structure involving lots of positive feedback and reinforcement and they react well to a relationship that provides this. Assertive/people types react positively to communication that is directed towards public acknowledgement of results. They are likely to be more flamboyant in dress and vocal style. They need public attention and acknowledgement.

These various types or styles and the characteristics I have given them are archetypal. Each style finds it difficult to communicate with the other. The passive/people person and the assertive/task person find communication, and therefore understanding, extremely difficult. The assertive/people person and the passive/task person are equally at odds with one another.

What you look for is the *primary intent* of the person with whom you are communicating. When you know what their needs are and you move slightly towards them in the way you communicate with them, they will move towards you. The possibility of a mutual understanding is greatly improved.

The essence behind effective communication lies in the extent to which you build some form of common ground between yourself and the person with whom you are communicating. The more

Communication styles

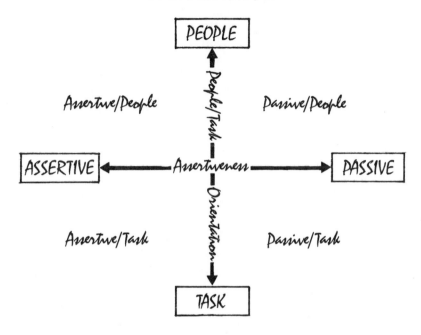

you focus on similarities and the less on differences, the better you 'communicate'.

Anatomy of communication

Studies show that the main impact of communication is non-verbal. In one study, some 55 per cent of people surveyed indicated that their understanding of communication derived from body language: posture, gesture and facial expression. A further 38 per cent were most affected by sound: tone, tempo and volume of voice. This left a meagre 7 per cent of people who were most impressed by the actual words that were spoken.[1]

The nature of our schooling leads us to believe that the words we use are the most important component of communication. This leads to great frustration, particularly among high-powered executives and professional people. We have now come to know that there must be a congruence between our words and our non-verbal messages. The key lies in a concept called 'pacing'—a basic communication skill which uses all elements of communication. It is a skill inherent in all good communicators.[2]

Pacing is following, rather than mimicking,[3] the non-verbal messages of your target person. For example, if your target is raising their voice, as might be the case with an assertive/people person, talking softly to them would highlight a difference. Using a level of sound just under their own minimises the difference and, along with pacing gesture or body movement, brings you into close 'rapport' with them. This rapport, this degree of conscious alikeness, aids the understanding and completeness of the communication.

As words are a large part of our conscious communication, it is as well to address some techniques for their use in verbal communication. Think how important this information is for communication by telephone. In these circumstances your voice plays a far greater role than we might imagine; how many of us pay enough attention to communicating on the telephone?

The first imperative in using the purely verbal aspect of communication is to be crystal clear about your intent. If the communication is about a regular event in your work environment, a check-list of the aspects you need to cover is useful in most circumstances.

There are three other keys to improved communication: recapitulation, reflective listening and responsibility.

The first, asking for a *recapitulation*, relates to *making* a verbal communication.

Once you have completed what you have to say, or are part way through a particularly long communication, pause and seek confirmation of what you have said. Ask what has been understood by the communication. The response will almost always involve different words to your own, although the words used will convey the extent of the understanding. If there is a gap in understanding, your subsequent conversation can focus on the gap, so that ultimately the communication is completed satisfactorily. You are then comfortable about the understanding and the value of the communication.

In my early working career, I discovered a communication issue relating to delegation. In my seminars I have discovered it is not at all uncommon. I learnt that, when defining a new task, I was often uncertain whether the other person really understood what I was saying to my full satisfaction.[4] The more I spoke, the more uncertain I became and the more difficult I found the confidence to 'let go' and delegate effectively. Once I discovered the value of recapitulation described above, delegation became simpler and my productivity improved enormously.

The reverse technique is known as *reflective listening*. Here, the listener watches for congruence between verbal and non-verbal signals. After that, all it takes is the occasional pause to reflect back to the other person what you think you have understood. For example, one particular consulting assignment of mine involved a large number of discussions, many of them lasting as long as 2 hours. At 15 or 20 minute intervals, at a suitable break in my listening, I said something along the lines of 'Now let me see if I have understood you fully . . .' and summarised in a minute or two the essence of what I had heard. This gave my colleagues a real sense of my understanding of what was being said and increased their confidence in the value of my contribution.

Using clarifying questions in key areas is also of value. 'What', 'when', 'where' and 'who' questions are more important than 'how' and 'why' questions. This is because 'what', 'when', 'where' and 'who' indicate genuine interest. 'How' is inappropriate before you have settled the detail of the instruction or communication, and 'why' can result in a defensive attitude.

Probably the most important issue in communication is *responsibility*—to accept 100 per cent responsibility for communication on a personal basis. I have noticed that the common approach on both sides of the communications fence is to unconsciously adopt a notional 50 per cent responsibility. 'I've made myself clear enough. You must be some kind of dummy not to understand it. What kind of a fool are you anyway!', or 'I heard you the first time. Why are you going over it all again? Do you take me for an idiot?'

When two people are communicating with one another and one or both are 100 per cent committed to their own responsibility in the process, the success rate in completing the understanding is much higher. I have a commitment to responsibility in communication in my personal guiding values. This reinforces my understanding about how important responsibility in effective communication really is.

Feedback

With complete communication, feedback is the most important aspect of high leverage work and it is also one of the least used. Feedback, when appropriately given, is as much a part of good management as goal setting and planning. It is integral to any program of performance improvement.

Feedback is telling the people who are important to you how you feel about what they have said or done. In a business context it means letting your colleagues know what you think of their performance.

Feedback is about reinforcing existing positive behaviour and performance, and building behaviour and performance in areas where improvement is necessary. It is about reinforcing high performance expectations, and encouraging people with whom you work to higher and higher levels of performance. Giving feedback in the context of genuine high positive expectations of performance is always seen as a positive contribution to subsequent performance. This is done by making positive, neutral and 'negative' comment on the performance you observe from the point of view of the person receiving the feedback. This may involve discussion about the effect of feedback and close observation of the results of the feedback. It is not done by critical carping commentary, nor is it done by making the other person feel in the wrong.

'You are too good to turn in this [specific] performance. Sit down with me and see if we cannot work out a way to do this to your normal high standard' is highly effective feedback. 'That was a stupid error. You must be a sandwich short of a picnic to turn in a performance like that', is not. Be tough on issues and 'soft' on people.

While conducting a consulting assignment, I spoke to one person who had just returned from maternity leave. She worked in an area of some technical difficulty and was desperate, quite literally, for feedback. She wanted to know what she had to learn and whether she was still capable of the demands of the job after her period away from work. Her supervisor was too busy with his own casework and had given her no feedback for more than 9 months. Her case files had banked up unattended in his pending tray. The officer became more and more concerned about her ability. She became highly demotivated and, eventually, found work of a totally different kind elsewhere in the organisation. She had trained and worked in her technical discipline for 15 years. In less than one-twentieth of that time her experience was substantially lost to her employer. With a little effort on the part of her supervisor, she could have been encouraged to re-establish her technical skills.

It is necessary to appreciate that positive feedback is an essential part of motivation. It is how we let people know that they are 'on target', that their performance is satisfactory, or that there are areas of their activity that could be improved. It is how we let them know that they are making progress on a task and, consequently, progress in their position and career.

Some people need feedback more frequently than others. Some situations require more feedback than others. Whatever the need, if you do not go out of your way to discover people, and friends, and family 'doing the right thing', you will not encourage the people in your life to develop to their fullest potential.

Providing full, positively reinforcing feedback, is one of the best uses you can make of your time. It is clearly high leverage activity.

THE PARETO PRINCIPLE

The Pareto Principle is another major way of assisting you to maintain focus on what is important. Taking the time to apply it to your work program and to the way you organise your day is another form of high leverage activity.

Dr Pareto, an Italian economist working in the late 19th century, discovered that 80 per cent of the wealth of Italy lay in the hands of 20 per cent of the Italian population. The Pareto Principle, or the 80/20 rule, has since been shown to have a much wider application. Alan Lakein[5] in his work on time management shows how the Pareto Principle applies to sales, production, sick leave, file usage, food recipes, expenditure and wardrobe usage. In short, the principle is universal. Everything you do is governed by it: 20 per cent of activity in anything you do will produce 80 per cent of your results in that area.

At first it seems a staggering perspective, almost unbelievable. Eighty per cent of your results, *in whatever you do*, derive from 20 per cent of your total effort. It is the reverse of the principle that is so horrifying. You spend 80 per cent of your time producing only 20 per cent of your results.

Test this important principle on something simple. Have a really close look at your wardrobe. You will almost certainly find shoes, suits, skirts, trousers, blouses, shirts and coats you no longer, or very rarely, wear. What proportion of your total wardrobe would these items constitute? If the proportion is much less than 80 per cent, you are truly unusual. Of course, you wear the remaining 20 per cent of your clothes the majority of the time.

In one organisation in which I worked, we undertook a Pareto analysis and learnt that some 90 per cent of our revenue derived

The Pareto Principle

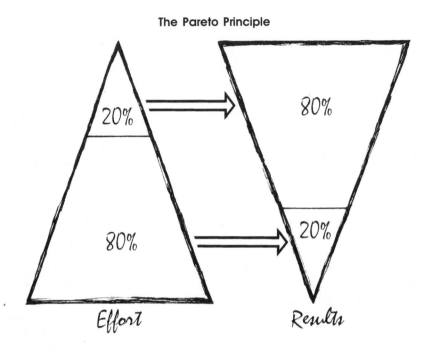

from 13 per cent of the client base. We were disturbed to discover that 87 per cent of our clients were responsible for such a meagre return (10 per cent). We decided that, as a result of this awareness, the organisation should direct some of this 'wasted' energy towards deciding which of its many non-performing clients could be encouraged to go elsewhere. There was some resistance to this decision. The least productive of our clients, were still responsible, as a whole, for some millions of dollars of revenue. Times were tough and we could ill afford to lose that level of revenue, or so we first thought. There was, moreover, a strong, historical attachment to some of those clients.

This reluctance to change was misplaced. The energy we previously spent on non-performing clients was considerable, more than 80 per cent of total activity. Once we started to shed these clients, we were able to devote more time to providing a better service to the level of clients we really wanted *and* to spend more highly productive time on marketing activities.

In another professional organisation in which I conducted a consulting assignment, I discovered that 23 per cent of the client base produced 78 per cent of gross revenue. I discovered that the last 40 per cent by number of the total client base produced 1.89 per cent of revenue. To rub salt into the wound, the realisation rate (revenue received as a proportion of invoices raised) for that 40 per cent was 58 per cent, which compared to the rate for the top 23 per cent of clients of 98.8 per cent. This discovery alone provided an opportunity for huge productivity and profit improvements.

We too often tend to hang on to the unproductive part of our organisation—product line, people or customers. We continue to devote a large portion of our energies to them in a mistaken belief that we cannot afford to do without them. The reality is that, when our energies are freed up from unproductive and unrewarding tasks, the time we would otherwise have spent on them is naturally and creatively drawn to activity that contributes more directly to our main purpose.

Go back to the simple example of our wardrobe. If we were to throw out 80 per cent of our clothes, the immediate result would be an obvious hole in our wardrobe. In a surprisingly short time, however, we would fill it with clothes more in accord with our current tastes and interests.

The lesson of the Pareto Principle is clear. Do what you can to support the clients, products, branches and people who produce your results for you and look very closely at those who do not. This last analysis should not be undertaken in an arbitrary way. In a law firm in which I worked, one of our 'non-performing' clients was the senior partner's mother-in-law. A number of clients were great referrers of quality work. A number of others we regarded as 'acorns', small clients with strong potential. We kept them all.

Identify the 80 per cent not producing results and look at each element in the context of your main business purpose. If your business focus is clear, what to do about each particular element of your non-performing activity will be apparent. You will also find that the degree of sensitivity you have to use to reduce the 'non-performers' will depend first on the nature of your business and second on your relationship with the targeted client. In some cases it can be done simply on the basis of price or quantity. In others it might involve some negotiation based on information about alternative suppliers for your product or service. Whatever the nature of your business, the process of shedding non-performing customers and clients can be accomplished with sensitivity and in a way that preserves a good relationship with your former client so that, when they do have business activity of a level appropriate to you, they will return. This certainly should be your objective.

I have concentrated here on applying the Pareto Principle to the relationship between revenue and customers or clients. This is largely because it is an obvious statistic for most organisations and an easy one to identify. The principle can be equally used to look at any activity in your organisation. A Pareto analysis may tell you something so significant about the way you conduct your affairs that you can make changes to your sales strategy immediately. It may, for example, tell you about the attention you could give to your principle customers. It may provide you with ways of trimming your sales force, prompt new ways of selling or provide you with solid information about the usefulness of different strategies for particular customers. It also applies, of course, with equal force to any area of your business activities: production, inquiry services, maintenance, safety incidence, finance, debtor control, personnel, marketing or advertising. There is no limit to the application of the principle.

You may have noticed that the Pareto Principle is continually applicable in that it does not stop with that first stage of analysis. Once you have identified that 20 per cent of your activity that produces 80 per cent of your results, you will find that the 80/20 rule applies all over again. Of that 20 per cent, 20 per cent again produces 80 per cent of your results! And so on, *ad infinitum*. This is another reason why the application of the principle is discretionary rather than absolute or arbitrary.

Another important application lies in the way each of us spends our day. Eighty per cent of our results derive directly from 1.5 to 2 hours each day!

Even in assembly-line work, it is true to say that the majority of results depend on the set-up, planning and maintenance of each operation. The quality of that preparation time, and the work done during it, bears directly on the output and quality of machine-running time.

The principle applies equally to a management context, although the dividing line is perhaps less clear. Thinking in Pareto terms is high leverage activity. Your effectiveness will depend, very substantially, on the extent to which you spend time on planning and organising your work activities and those of your team or organisation. Putting the Pareto Principle to work by spending two hours each day (20 per cent of your day) on longer term thinking and action adds considerable value.

EFFICIENCY AND EFFECTIVENESS

It is an important part of improved performance to keep a clear understanding of the very real distinction between efficiency and effectiveness. In my consulting work, I have noticed that this distinction is not always understood or maintained.

'Efficiency' is 'doing your work right'; 'effectiveness' is 'doing the right work'. Effectiveness is about focus—doing things that contribute to your main purpose, your goals and objectives. Efficiency only has value if it is related to work that contributes directly to a conscious desired outcome. Efficiency is not an end in itself. There is little value in being efficient—doing what you do well—if you are doing something that does not contribute to your goals or to those of your organisation. To be truly effective you must first choose the right task on which to work. At this point, and this alone, does efficiency have a value.

In the course of my work, sometimes I have noticed work being undertaken on a task, sometimes by a number of people, when it was no longer important for that task to be done. When the task was first assigned it was an effective use of resources. The relevance of the task or its effectiveness had shifted over time. The initial purpose may have been met or the circumstance that determined it may have changed. Whatever efficiency had developed in the task had absolutely no current value.

This phenomenon applies particularly in larger organisations, although smaller ones are not 'clean' in this respect. It is a particular malaise of large public bureaucracies, where a specific legislative demand requires the activity long after the need for it has gone. No one thinks to change the legislation. I would rather see my employees working inefficiently on something that contributes to the goals of my organisation, than to see them working efficiently on something that does not contribute directly to those goals.

Having the distinction between effectiveness and efficiency clearly in mind is an excellent way to keep focus on your major outcomes. This applies equally to individuals, teams and organisations.

ANALYSIS OF WORK TASKS

There are two distinct ways of categorising work tasks. The first is by importance and urgency; the second is by length and complexity. It is helpful to have these distinctions in mind as we go about our work.

Urgency and importance

The distinction between urgency and importance is often blurred, if not in our minds, then in the way we act. The activity of many managers and professional people with whom I have worked often shows a tendency to equate urgency with importance. If it looks or sounds urgent, it must be important! Important, however, means it is part of your purpose, part of your commitment to your goals and objectives. It may or may not be urgent. Urgent means that someone, for some reason, thinks it should be done *now*! It may or may not be important.

To know that you are working on tasks that are important to you and your organisation is a major source of personal motivation, satisfaction and general wellbeing. The obverse is also true: if you direct your energies to tasks that ultimately do not contribute anything to you or your organisation, you are likely to be much less enthusiastic about, and committed to, your work.

Tasks that are *urgent and important* must get done and generally do without a great deal of conscious thought as to planning their execution. It is in this area—of the *urgent and important* task—that the concern for improved productivity lies. It is important that *urgent and important* tasks constitute as small a proportion of your day as possible. Set them into a planning framework that makes sense of your ability to react effectively to the demands of such work. These are 'priority A' tasks and it is useful to aim at them constituting no more than 20 per cent of your planned workload.

To spend a majority of your day on *urgent and important* work can project you into 'crisis management'. This may add to your own sense of being needed on the job, but it in no way contributes to your long-term effectiveness, nor does it contribute to your good health. The aim is to plan your workload in a way which allows you to devote no more time to real crises or emergencies than is absolutely necessary. I once worked with a manager who thrived on crises, so much so that he created them. Whatever it was it was a crisis. He liked nothing better than to say: 'I can't talk to you now, Pete, I have a crisis on my hands.' His style was infectious. The people around him often became distracted from their own priorities, much to the general ineffectiveness of the group.

54

The urgency/importance matrix

	Urgent	Non urgent
Important	'A' Priority 20%	'B' Priority 60%
Unimportant	'C' Priority 20%	

By definition, *urgent and unimportant* tasks should be 'priority C' tasks. Again aim to spend no more than 20 per cent of your time on them. Unhappily it seems all too easy to react to the urgency of a task rather than to properly assess its real importance, and there is a tendency for this category of work to escalate in proportion.

Once you have decided a task is *urgent and unimportant*, it is useful to communicate with the person from whom the sense of urgency derives. This provides an opportunity for the real importance of the task to be assessed. This works well in an organisation in which you wish to maintain good working relationships, or in a situation in which good customer or client relationships are important. When this is done you may decide to rely on your own sense of priorities and decline the task. A clear focus on what is important is, of course, absolutely essential.

My work and consulting experience shows that 'urgency' is often a reflection of low expectations. When someone is not expected to meet a reasonable time commitment, the due date is escalated to 'urgent' just to make sure the task gets done. The way to combat this is to build a reputation for meeting your commitments. Over time this takes a lot of the sting out of colleagues and customers who insist on the urgency of a task.

In my seminars I have often found that there is a resistance to change among employees in relation to clients, customers and supervising managers. Instead, there is a strong desire to react instantly to a client or boss *irrespective of the real need*. I work in a client-oriented industry and service is the *sine qua non* of my business. When I react in an emergency to one or more clients without properly discussing the task and assessing its overall importance to me and my client, I find that I am not 'at home' to look after another client where the need is truly important. As in all things, balance is important.

I have also discovered that my clients' main need is to be heard, to know that their concern is seen to be important, and that they are valued. It is always interesting to discover that, as soon as this has been established, the urgency dissipates. Discussion about a commitment to handle the work to an agreed timetable can then proceed.

Certainly, there are genuine emergencies. The skill is to correctly identify them rather than assume that urgency equates with importance.

As far as the impatient senior manager is concerned, I can only suggest that your responsibility extends to managing upwards *in the interests of your own improved performance*. This requires patience, tact and open communication. You may have to keep a priority list handy and talk with your boss about the effect on existing priorities of reacting immediately to 'urgency'. The words you use and the way you go about the exercise will have to work for you. There is little sense in beating your head against a brick wall and my experience tells me that few people try. Mostly the 'urgency' derives from a sense of 'This is the way you have to act to get things done in this place'. Even the most difficult senior manager will want to be reminded of the truism: 'If everything is urgent, nothing is urgent'.

The big contributor to loss of productivity is the extent to which you allow yourself to be distracted by tasks that are *neither urgent nor important*. The tendency for them to take up a significant amount of your time is based on the internal satisfaction you have in completion of any task. This accounts for the time you spend shuffling and reshuffling papers; prioritising and reprioritising the unimportant; doing routine things that can be better and more appropriately handled through delegation.

Spending time on *non-urgent and unimportant* activity is wholly unproductive. Delegate some tasks[6] and only address the remaining tasks if you have no alternative and certainly not before tackling anything else that is important. Organising your tasks in this way is high leverage activity.

Parkinson's Second Law states: 'The time spent on any matter is usually inversely proportional to its importance!'[7] If we ignore this, our productivity is bound to suffer.

The most significant category of task is work that is *important and non-urgent*. Tasks in this category tend to be left unattended until they become *urgent and important*. At this point you have no choice other than to do them . . . and to hell with your partner, your children, and that game of golf! It is well to address the *important and non-urgent* tasks by planning them into your schedule of activity, in such a way that they are addressed before they become urgent. Check their importance and, once confirmed, give them an implementation schedule that works. These are 'priority B' tasks and you should aim for them to take up close to 60 per cent of your total workload.

It is important to notice that the *important and non-urgent* task tends to be the kind of activity that has a major direct bearing on your personal (and organisational) performance. Planning, ideas generation, organising, training, and, probably most important of all, communications in general and feedback in particular, are important and often non-urgent tasks, and, as such, *high leverage activity.*

When we do not plan properly for the appropriate execution of the *important and non-urgent* tasks, they become *important and urgent* and therefore add to the level of crisis management we experience. This has its inevitable effect on performance, sometimes encouraging major omissions and errors of judgement. The cost to you in not putting aside this time is considerable.

In summary, the danger of an unplanned working life is that the *unimportant and non-urgent* tasks may dominate your existence and prevent proper attention being directed to the *important and non-urgent*. If this occurs you find yourself dealing with one crisis after another. Crises may be unavoidable once in a while; they should not be allowed to dominate your life.

Eliminate the *unimportant and non-urgent* work and properly plan the accomplishment of the *important and non-urgent*. Then you are well on your way to higher levels of performance.

Length and complexity

It is valuable to understand how length and complexity of a task affect productivity. For the most part handling all but the *long-term/complex* tasks presents very little concern. All that is necessary is to ensure that they are put into an appropriate order of importance and that the *number* of tasks does not distract you from the *long-term/complex* tasks of importance.

The *long-term complex* task is a major distraction and inhibitor of personal productivity improvements, and can only be usefully dealt with by proper analysis, planning and detailed scheduling. The difficulty in addressing large and relatively complex tasks lies in an inability to visualise the completed task and the process necessary to reach that target. For the lucky few this is relatively easy. For most it is difficult and we tend to close our mind to it, creatively avoiding almost anything to do with it until we have a crisis on our hands.

With *long-term complex* tasks you may find that breaking the task into smaller, more readily 'do-able' sub-tasks is a useful exercise. Identifying and dealing with each small sub-task facilitates an appreciation of the place of the sub-task in the overall task. Moreover, a considerable momentum is created towards completing the overall task when focus is concentrated on the accomplishment of its smaller components.

Identifying each sub-task, or group of interrelated sub-tasks, can be scheduled separately into acceptable periods of time. Also quite valuable is making each small sub-task part of your personal recognition and feedback procedure.

A WORK AUDIT

Many standard texts on time management strongly recommend an audit of the actual time you spend over a minimum period of a fortnight. This process, it is suggested, should be repeated every 6 months or so to monitor improvements and to suggest further adjustments to behavioural patterns. I am happy to confess that I am somewhat ambivalent about a work audit, largely because I know from experience that very few people ever actually complete one.

The advantage of the audit is that it is normally quite arresting. When you discover how much time you actually spend on

A sample work audit form

Date	Meetings	Meeting preparation	Travel/waiting	Telephone calls – OUT	Telephone calls – IN	Research	Planning	Counselling/coaching	Feedback				
7:30													
7:45													
8:00													
8:15													
8:30													
8:45													
9:00													
9:15													
9:30													
9:45													
10:00													
10:15													
10:30													
10:45													
11:00													
11:15													
11:30													
1.													
1:30													
1:45													
2:00													
2:15													
2:30													
2:45													
3:00													
3:15													
3:30													
3:45													
4:00													
4:15													
4:30													
4:45													
5:00													
5:15													
5:30													
5:45													
6:00													
6:15													
6:30													

the telephone, in meetings, or in dealing with interruptions, it can be quite a shock.

A simple form can easily be designed by dividing your day by quarter or half-hour segments (see page 59). The form records quite simply how you spend your day. It tells you at the end of a fortnight how much of your time you have spent on telephone calls, meetings, interviews, writing, thinking, dictating, and social and other interruptions. The form should allow space for you to indicate the value you place on each recorded occurrence. You are then in a position to see how well you distribute your time on priority tasks, and can also see quite clearly the areas in which you can make some improvement.

Other things to look for are:

- that *portion* of the day which is most productive;
- those *activities* you undertook that produced major results;
- those *activities* you undertook that were not productive; and
- those *portions of particular activities* that were most effective and those that were not.

A work audit analysis such as this, followed by an ordered application of the Pareto Principle, provides one of the most important keys to improved performance.

The following chapter is designed to assist you in applying specific techniques in order to better manage telephone calls and the various other forms of distractions that occur. Some of your activities may not be fully productive, although they may also be important to you in terms of your chosen lifestyle. It is vital that these activities reflect a conscious choice on your part.

If undertaking an audit works for you, consider doing it at regular intervals, say, of 6 or 12 months. If you are uncomfortable about it, try it once just for the motivation to make the necessary change.

KEY MESSAGES FROM CHAPTER 3

- *Identify high leverage activities appropriate to your role (goal setting and planning, organising, training, communications and feedback) and ensure that you spend quality time on them at least once a day.*

- *Put aside time each day—not at a regular time—to focus on communication and feedback to the people to whom you relate closely.*

Do this at the work place and at home. Know that it won't always work out the way you thought it would and that next time it will be easier and more effective.

- *Be clear about your training needs and those of your team. Make sure it is appropriate training and that a full evaluation occurs. Counsel your colleagues before and after a training session. Make training a proactive exercise based on the needs of your team and the development of the individuals within it.*

- *Undertake a regular Pareto analysis of your work and that of your team. Make sure that low productive activity is assessed for its continuing relevance to your goals and objectives.*

- *Set aside 1 to 2 hours each day for uninterrupted Pareto time so that you can concentrate on high leverage activity—activity that is important and non–urgent.*

- *Think about the value of a one-off work task audit in order to properly assess how you spend your time. Use the results creatively. Involve your team in any changes you decide to make.*

CHAPTER 4

Staying on track 2

*We have left undone those things which we ought
to have done; and we have done those things
which we ought not to have done.*

The Book of Common Prayer

The previous chapters covered a number of principles of human
behaviour which govern how we operate as individuals, managers and team leaders. Applying these principles will result in
enormous benefits to your personal productivity. You are now
able to ensure you are working on those things that create major
impact for you. You will be able to direct your attention to your
work in ways that keep you moving forward in a creative way.
You will be able to make better use of the people with whom you
work, and you will develop new ways of working which dramat-
ically improve the use you make of your time.

Here now are some additional suggestions for avoiding such
major time wasters as procrastination, interruptions and misuse
of the telephone.

DEALING WITH PROCRASTINATION

The experience of my seminars and consulting work suggests
quite strongly that procrastination is a major concern for many
people, at least in some aspects of their work. The paradox is that
procrastination in more a reflection of lack of focus than an
accurate reflection of actual performance.

As a high performance person, you are reading this book to
further improve your performance. It would be unusual to find
someone interested in doing so who was not open to new ideas
involving personal growth through change. This is, after all, one

of the hallmarks of top achievers. Paradoxically, it is only the high performance sophisticated operator who is concerned about procrastination. It is only when you work in a complex performance-oriented environment that issues about procrastination occur.

In my consulting work and in the feedback I receive in my seminars on this subject, I have found a preoccupation with the negative feelings about delaying key tasks. Too often, moving a task from one day's schedule to another is called procrastination, whereas it may, in reality, be a sound management decision based on the emerging priorities of the moment. It could be that, on closer examination, a task requires information or input from other sources not immediately available. It is far better to re-schedule the task to a time when it can be dealt with more effectively. This is not procrastination.

True procrastination is putting something off to another day when you know it should be done now. A sound management decision based on relative priorities is not procrastination. Review your work and acknowledge the tasks you complete on a daily basis and see the shift from 'procrastination' to achievement.

Procrastination has two main causes, both of which you create for yourself: apathy and anxiety.

Apathy is a condition characteristic of most cases of procrastination, whatever its true underlying cause. The first step in dealing with it involves 'deciding' not to do it and looking at the cost to you of not doing it. If this creates a real problem for you, it is likely that it is not apathy that is causing procrastination. You may then consider one of the ways of dealing with procrastination set out below.

If it does not create a problem or concern for you, or if the cost is so slight as to be manageable, leave it permanently off your agenda. It is not a question of procrastination, just a matter of priorities and overall importance.

Anxiety, often subconscious anxiety, that accompanies real procrastination is a fear of a future event. After you have finally completed a task on which you have procrastinated, you discover how much less difficult or worrisome it really is. Our after-the-event lessons are that the task is far less of a concern than we imagined. The earth does not disappear from under our feet, the sun always rises the next day, and we receive the plaudits of our colleagues for completing the task. We never seem to really learn the lesson of this experience. This is why I say anxiety is irrational[1] in this context, however understandable it is. There is also an irrational, although nonetheless very real, fear of openly expressing ourselves. Anxiety may also derive from an unusually complex task, something for which you have no direct experience, or from a requirement to present a colleague or client with information they may not appreciate.

The following suggestions for beating procrastination deal either directly with the fear or provide ways of addressing the event while overriding the fear in some way. They are offered as a smorgasbord of potential 'cures' from which you may select the two or three which will work for you.

Bite the bullet

One effective way of breaking out of an anxiety state when anticipating a difficult or distasteful task, is to 'bite the bullet'. Get on with it. Your only surprise will be how easy it was and how much better you feel. This applies to all unpleasant tasks such as admitting an error or failure to perform, denying a request or cancelling an order.

Set priorities

A conscious sense of priorities makes it very difficult to procrastinate. Activity is automatically generated on key tasks and key outcomes. Allowing unimportant activities and irrelevant 'commitments' to clutter your mind is destructive and diminishes your level of achievement accordingly. Devote your energy and enthusiasm to tasks that are important to you and procrastination will not be an issue.

Key task

This technique involves identifying the key or critical elements of a major task about which you have some degree of 'anxiety'. Once the key elements are clear, focus your mind on action directed at them. Identify action steps and program the commitments to particular activity into your diary system.

Relate this to the 'salami' or 'Swiss cheese' technique. Divide the task into 'do-able' chunks and address them one at a time. This is based on the notion that no one, as far as I can tell, is comfortable about the thought, much less the practice, of eating a whole salami or Swiss cheese in one sitting. It is much more comfortable and satisfactory to divide it into bite-size chunks.

Next action step

This is a more sophisticated technique, akin to the 'key task' technique. Each task you address, however complex, is made up of single steps which together constitute the completed task. The technique, therefore, involves identifying the 'next single action step' needed to begin moving towards task achievement. This will almost always be something simple and straightforward: identifying a telephone number; booking a room or flight; identifying a supplier, and so on.

A colleague of mine wanted to establish his own business. For many months he researched and planned his activity until it became apparent to me that he was procrastinating; certainly there was a justifiable fear in making such a large step. Eventually he decided to identify his 'next action step', which was to contact a real estate agent in the area where he wanted to operate. Once this was done, the energy flow on the establishment of the business was unstoppable.

The reason this technique works is that the commitment to action is made on something that is readily achievable and breaks any fear you may have of the task. This, in turn, allows you to take the required action and so move towards ultimate task achievement. Once you have taken a single step, another appears as if by magic. Before you know it, there is a momentum about your activity and a record of achievement that carries you forward almost effortlessly.

End-result imagery/creative visualisation

This technique is also simple and straightforward. It is described in detail in chapter 1. Use it to imagine the end product or outcome of the task about which you are procrastinating. If your image is vital and real, it will draw you forward to a positive result.

Delayed gratification

This is a simple yet powerful technique directed at avoiding procrastination in our daily activities. Put simply, it means prioritising your work each day in the normal way by doing the tasks that are of most interest to you last. Ensure that they are important and that they contribute to your major goals in a meaningful way. Do not fall into the trap of allowing 'interesting' to divert you from what is important. This means that you do all the important tasks that *have* to be done, especially those that do not really interest you, first. You are then able to follow them with those tasks that provide some special value. If you do the most interesting tasks first you run the risk of putting the uninteresting and important tasks off until the next day.

In one organisation where I worked, a colleague placed the most interesting task he had for each day in full sight of him, yet out of reach. He reported that this drew him forward very productively through the routine tasks as he knew he could spend quality (guilt-free) time on something that really challenged him.

Practised routinely, delayed gratification has a much wider application than dealing specifically with procrastination. M Scott Peck, for example, in his best-selling work, describes the practice of delayed gratification as being the hallmark of top performers generally.[2]

Balance sheet/diary

The use of a 'balance sheet' or 'diary' is an effective way of dealing directly with the fear or anxiety associated with procrastination.

The balance sheet approach is best suited to the more analytical style of person, the diary to more 'emotional' people. It is very straightforward: divide a page into two vertical halves. On the left side write down the *benefits* of completing the task on time and to a specified standard. On the right side write down the *problems* that will occur for you if you do not complete it. The advantages of getting the task done always outweigh the costs of not doing it.

To use the diary technique, write down in diary form how you *feel* about the task. Describe your fears and from where they derive. Describe your hopes, wishes and dreams. Consider what is needed to feel more comfortable about starting on the task. Describe the advantages of completing the task and how good you will feel. This translates an internal anxiety into tangible form and you have a way of dealing more effectively with its irrationality.

I used this technique at a very difficult period of my life. I had been quite devastated by a marriage break-up and had difficulty focusing on my work. I spent hours writing about how I felt, what the break-up of my marriage meant to me and what my future options might be. Within a very short period of time I was back on track, enthusiastic about my work and my future. I had to force myself to use the diary technique and by doing so, it took me out of a mould and opened me up to new ways of looking at my issue. If you are task or analytically-oriented as I am, you may find it useful to use the diary technique in addition to the balance sheet model when faced with particularly intractable areas of procrastination.

A more structured and very valuable method for turning procrastination, and any other form of personal or corporate 'adversity' to more effective responses, may be derived from the work of Albert Ellis. A very useful structure based on Ellis's work is contained in a recent book by Martin Seligman[3] and this is discussed in some detail in section 2 of this book, 'Understanding Change in Self and Others'.

Avoiding perfection

One of the most common ways in which anxiety manifests itself is in an unwillingness to attempt any task unless you are certain that you can do it to perfection. This causes you to put the task off altogether or leads you to take an unconscionably long time to complete it. Deal with this by addressing minimum or optimum standards of completion for the task. Make sure you understand them completely and the reasons for them, as well as the time constraints involved in the particular task. Discuss the standard you reach with your colleagues and do this openly and honestly, disclosing all your concerns about the outcome.

Make notes of the resulting commitments. Write statements for the standard of completion for each part of the task, and build the sub-task and completion date into your diary and re-submission systems. Create a support structure within your team to assist the acknowledgement of all achievements.

Time and quality of standard of output are very often trade-offs in management tasks. Describing the standard of completion allows a more realistic time frame for completion and assists in moving away from the need for perfection.

Some tasks may have to be completed to a very high, even perfect, standard. These are very rare indeed and often have a scientific, technical or legal element to them. Moving away from perfectionism towards (high) specific standards of performance will afford you considerable gains in productivity.

Setting deadlines

A useful way of beating procrastination is to set milestones and expected completion times, and make commitments about them in your diary or re-submission system. This provides focus and allows you to move forward towards completion. Supplement this with end result imagery in order to boost your determination to meet the milestones and complete on target.

Know that circumstances do change and you will need to adapt to these changes in a flexible and responsible way. This is sound management; delay through indecision is procrastination. It is also sound management to communicate milestones, and any changes made to them, to all who share a project with you.

HANDLING INTERRUPTIONS

Applying the key principles of this book will provide you with a framework in which interruptions can be handled readily and responsively. After all, some interruptions are welcome. They may form a useful and timely relief from intense concentration. They may bring you essential and relevant information about the task on which you are working. You may also see it as important to be able to respond with care to interruptions from colleagues who are in some form of genuine stress. This is an appropriate part of good team building.

In short, you can plan, or make arrangements or allowances for interruptions that are important for you. You can also be responsible and caring about those that you cannot handle precisely at the moment they occur. The key is to organise your day and manage your workload by retaining a clear focus on what is important. Unwanted interruptions are a major time waster. This is not only because of the amount of time spent on the interruption it is also because of the cumulative time you spend regathering your thoughts so you can go back to the precise point you were at when the interruption occurred. A 2 hour exercise can extend into days because of interruptions.

Telephone interruptions

Telephone interruptions are particularly damaging because they are unpredictable. There is no way of assessing their importance when they ring; *urgency is easily mistaken for importance.*

Planning and controlling your use of the telephone is probably more important than other aspects of your work. It is certainly the basis of effectively controlling telephone interruptions. It is done primarily through screening your calls and the most effective way to do this is by developing a full understanding with the people who work closely with you. If you have the advantage of a good secretary or personal assistant, complete communication is essential. Be clear about what calls, if any, should be allowed through and what kind of response to give to those calls that are screened out. Full communication with your secretary or personal assistant will often allow them to deal effectively with a large proportion of your incoming telephone calls, thus cutting down on interruptions considerably. Keep your personal assistant constantly informed of the most important aspects of your work. Also let your assistant know of any expected calls and their likely nature, and provide possible responses.

In all my work and consulting experience I have never seen the trust that underpins this level of communication misplaced. The converse is true. When full trust is given, loyalty and commitment increase and your total productivity improves considerably.

If you do not have a secretary or personal assistant, ad hoc communication at critical times with a telephonist or receptionist is essential. A number of other options are available:

- Communicate fully with nearby work colleagues at key times, and be sure to return the favour when they want to be uninterrupted.
- Use an answering device whenever there are periods during which you cannot be disturbed. Be sure to return all those calls as soon as you can. When you are away from your office for prolonged periods make sure you have someone taking clear messages and able to respond with a holding acknowledgement.
- Arrange to have your phone forwarded to another person who is willing to receive your calls.
- In special circumstances move to another office or quiet place where you can work completely undisturbed. Make sure at least one person knows where you are and under what general circumstances you may be contacted.

Personal interruptions

Personal callers are a little more difficult, largely because of our unwillingness to 'confront' people generally. There are a number of things you can do in the way of office design and layout to minimise the possibility of personal interruptions or drop-ins.

An example of poor office design

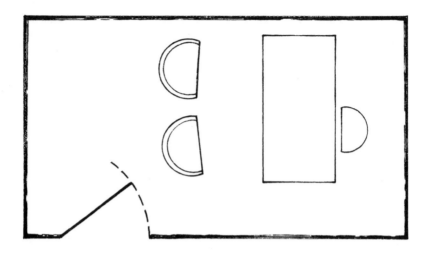

This will depend on the space and furniture available to you. For example, avoid having a series of inviting lounge chairs at the entrance to your office. When your caller can sink into a chair before you can react, you have no power over the interruption. This is a common characteristic of many offices, actively encouraging interruptions through ease of eye contact and tacit invitation. A typical poor design is set out above.

The room designs on page 71 give some idea of the options available in reducing eye contact and making interruptions less likely.

Using these or similar patterns optimises your control over personal callers. They reduce the chance of colleagues catching your eye as they walk by your office. If a colleague does break into your concentration, you are close enough to the doorway to rise and talk to them standing. An office layout which permits you to rise at the entrance to the office when you receive a caller firmly places you, in most circumstances, in a position where you can assess the situation. You may retain the stand up 'let's get to business' posture, or you may decide whether to extend that into a friendly discussion in which you sit with them away from a desk or in more formal mode at the desk. If the discussion is most usefully held at a desk, the diagrams on page 72 indicate more productive ways of using the desk than sitting in an authoritarian way across the desk from your colleague.

Examples of effective office layouts

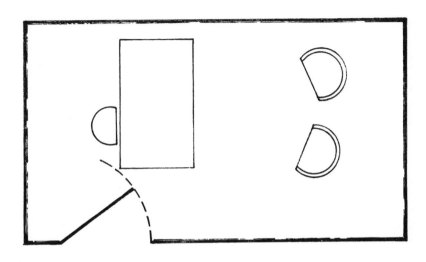

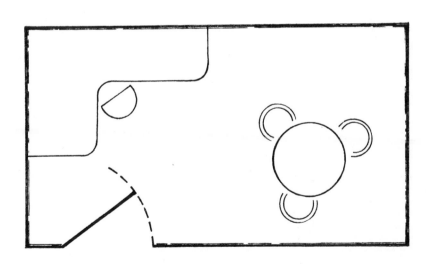

Examples of productive meeting seating

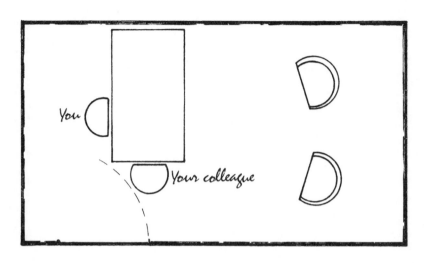

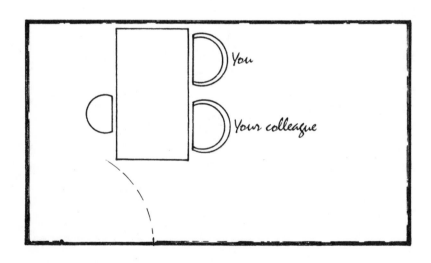

Whatever the nature of the discussion you have begun, you would be wise to get to the point of the visit or discussion at once. Set an agenda and agree on a time limit for your discussion. This takes no more firmness or consideration of your visitor and of yourself than is required in saying 'no', which after all may well be the bottom line at any one time.

SAYING 'NO'

The clearer you are about what is important to you and the steps you should take to reach them, the easier it is to say 'no'. Without this, you may be less discerning in the kinds of things you permit to intrude on your concentration. I am not recommending inflexibility; quite the reverse. Knowing what is important presents you with clearer choices about whether to say 'yes' or 'no'. Compare this with the principles underlying the tea ceremonies of the Chinese and Japanese cultures as well as those of the martial arts. The total concentration involved in the practice of these ancient arts is the very basis of the freedom of thought and expression which renders their art possible. The most important thing in saying 'no' is to be firm and caring when doing so. Few are offended by a polite understanding refusal, based squarely on a real empathy with the inquirer and an honest and open declaration of your position. If the interruption you are rejecting is based on organisational or personal concerns, it is always appropriate to make an early appointment to discuss the matter.

To accept a task or conversation of no value often involves resentment of the intrusion you have allowed. This is always reflected back to your colleague or customer in a number of non-verbal ways. A firm and caring 'no' will do less damage than a much resented 'yes'.

You gain more respect through honest, open firmness. Trying not to hurt another's feelings, or working under the mistaken belief that you have to be accessible to all people at all times to be an effective manager or leader, is far from productive. An effective leader is one who allocates time well and who achieves this on the basis of a firm respect for the dignity of the people with whom he or she relates.

73

USING THE TELEPHONE TO YOUR ADVANTAGE

There are a number of key points to be aware of when using a telephone. Despite the obviousness of these points, it is my observation in the consulting work that I have done that most people ignore them most of the time, much to their distinct disadvantage. The key is to be always conscious that your telephone is a business tool rather than a social tool, or some mixture of the two. A useful habit is to declare an agenda at the outset of a call. This could cover topic, outcome and time you expect to take on the call. Start by logging incoming and outgoing telephone calls each day for a fortnight, using the form similar to the 'Personal work audit' set out in the previous chapter. Repeat this every 6 months or so and observe the improvements you make.

CONCLUSION

To become more effective, to achieve more in the time available to you, is rarely a matter of making dramatic changes. Improved performance is more likely to be based on a constant attention to incremental changes. Part of this is your constant awareness of just how you spend your time. This awareness, measured against a knowledge of what is important, provides the basis for making incremental advances in performance, which result in a significant impact over time.

KEY MESSAGES FROM CHAPTER 4

- *As soon as you become aware that you are genuinely procrastinating about something that is important to you, assess it carefully and apply one of the techniques in this chapter.*

- *Interruptions are substantially within your control. When you put aside time to concentrate on work of value to you, make sure you have done what you can to limit the interruptions.*

- *Demand respect for your time and your work. Practice saying 'no!' out of a strong personal sense of what is important to you. Do this with respect for the dignity of the people affected.*

CHAPTER 5

Building a team
of champions

*Leaders create a place to go, a place to be. They
have commitment, passion, zest, energy, care,
love, and enthusiasm that they readily,
unashamedly express. And that is their
distinction.*

Tom Peters and Nancy Austin,
A Passion for Excellence [1]

Building a team of champions is first about vision and, second,
about the twin skills that underpin vision in putting runs on the
board:

- the technical skills of management, and
- the interpersonal skills of developing and encouraging excellent working relationships among team members.

The two are in many respects interrelated. The focus on the
personal organisation aspects of management skills underpins this
discussion on building a team of champions.

The people with whom you work are your most valuable
resource. Your own performance depends on creating and maintaining an environment in which your colleagues can grow and
be truly effective in their own right. The real test of your skill as
a leader of people is to be utterly fearless about developing them.
If this means running the 'risk' of having them out-perform you
and develop beyond you, so be it.

This chapter is about the skills of leadership. It is about the
value of good communication in building high performance
teams. It is about motivation, high positive expectations, and
well-balanced rewards and recognition systems.

THE VALUE OF COMMUNICATION IN
LEADING PEOPLE [2]

For a large part of my life I searched for a magic button which, when pressed, would make my life 'work' for me. My life has only 'worked' from the time when I realised that there was no such button. I now know the value of depending directly on my own internal resources and strength. I accept full responsibility for my life and I have stopped blaming 'fate' for my mistakes and 'luck' for my successes.[3] I accept that taking action is the only reliable way forward, even when it is risky and there is a degree of fear and uncertainty. I also accept the value of open communication. Indeed the nearest I have come to discovering that magic button is my belief in communication with integrity.[4]

I now know that an abiding characteristic of all high performance people is the quality of their communication. The key to this is openness and integrity. These qualities provide a sound basis for the trust that enhances growth on a personal, team and corporate level. Trust is the basis of the learning organisation[5] and the long-term corporate vitality with which it is so closely associated.

The quality of communication in your team determines how well you work together. Creativity, motivation and the willingness to take responsible risks are all based on quality of communication. It also determines how quickly minor difficulties within your team are resolved, thus preventing them from escalating into disruptive antagonism. Quality communication determines the ease with which your team coordinates its activity with related teams inside and outside your organisation. It determines the extent to which your team can develop into a truly high performance group and also the speed of that development.

Quality communication leads directly to effective relationships and to shared visions and values, and this in turn leads to improved performance.

Communication is about understanding. It is about appreciating the work of others and letting them know of your own desire for direct appreciation. It is about clarification, and about lifting performance through genuine high positive expectations.

Communicate assertively and be open about your reactions and your feelings. Communicate with responsibility, accepting that you are responsible for the way you feel about what occurs and the way you react. Communicate about the way you feel about failure and success, and how you feel when a member of your team does not perform to your expectations. Do it without making your colleague feel in the wrong. Be positive and supportive, particularly with those close to you.

For many, communication at this level of intensity is unnerving. It breaks patterns of pre-existing behaviour and this causes its own difficulties. There are no formulas for communicating more effectively other than to do it. In 'doing it' you will feel uncomfortable, even ridiculous. Go ahead anyway, knowing that you may muff it a number of times, and that, as you practice, you become better. As you improve and your communication becomes more effective, your confidence will grow and the results will begin to show.

Make a start by letting your colleagues know that you plan to improve the level and integrity of your communication. Let them know that you will be awkward at first and that you may ruffle a few feathers. Seek an understanding that communication is not complete until they have had a chance to respond to what you say. Tell them their responses have your full support. Work towards creating an atmosphere where honest and open communication is safe for your team.

We now begin to deal with building effective relationships, based on high quality communication, with your colleagues and team members.[6]

BUILDING HIGH PERFORMANCE PEOPLE—MOTIVATION

Regardless of the size of your team, building your close colleagues into high performance people is substantially a function of motivation and expectation.[7] Motivation, the first of these two critical factors, is essentially an internal phenomenon, a matter of personal choice, however much environmental conditions may make it easier for you to decide on a particular course of action.

This is illustrated in an exaggerated way by the following analogy. If a bank robber places a live, cocked gun at your head and demands money, you have a choice. You may give the robber the money, or you may refuse and run the risk of forfeiting your life. It is your choice and you must wear the consequences of that choice.

Similarly, your boss may say to you that you have a choice of lifting your performance in a particular respect, or leave the organisation. Your reaction to the choice is entirely your own. A friend of mine was given a choice between improving her call rate in a sales and consulting environment and taking a salary cut. In other words, her salary was to become based on performance. She wanted to meet the performance targets and stay in the position. As far as I could tell, her employer also wanted her to stay. Rather than make the changes necessary to improve her sales performance, she chose to leave.

Her conscious desire to lift her performance was outweighed by her unconscious fear of not making sufficient calls to justify the anticipated improved performance.[8] Her employer did not understand the cause of her fear or make it easy for her to meet the challenge he had given her. The choice to rise to a challenge was entirely hers. Her employer could have provided a number of environmental factors which would have made her choice easier. His role as a team leader is to manage his team's environment so as to enhance the likelihood of each person's choice being exercised in favour of improved performance.

A motivational environment is one that arouses, channels and sustains positive behaviour. The two key elements of a motivational environment are technical competence in a position, and the interest a person has in using that competence. Compare this to Wilfred Jarvis' notion of the leader's dilemma.[9] He explains that the main task of a leader in the relationship with the leader's colleagues is to decide what level of control to impose. The choice should be based on 'job efficiency' for a particular task, deriving in turn from the colleague's productive skills and creative energies. Once the nature of the task is clear and the job efficiency understood, the most appropriate level of control becomes obvious. (Jarvis' work is an important and sophisticated model of leadership based on a lifetime's search for fundamental truths about the nature of the relationships between people.)

Technical competence in the tasks a person is asked to perform, is a basic necessity. It may relate to the requirements of the position as a whole or, only to certain aspects of it. Whatever the degree of technical competence, this will have a strong effect on 'motivation' to perform. Motivation includes 'motivational environment', meaning those things for which you as a manager or team leader have responsibility in the process of encouraging your people to higher levels of performance.

Understanding the level of technical competence, and coaching and supporting your colleague to improved competence in order to meet the demands of a position, is therefore important. It is probably the easiest aspect of motivation to identify and certainly the easiest to remedy once it has been identified.

The other important aspect of motivation is your colleagues' interest in applying their skills. This is an area less amenable to quick, easy solutions. There are a number of key factors which can affect your ability to motivate your team:

- clarity about direction and participation in deciding on team and corporate vision, values and objectives;
- understanding the nature of the work place itself, the resources available to do the job, the standard of supervision and the degree to which obstacles that hinder effective and efficient work are removed;
- the degree of cooperation members of the team receive from one another and the extent to which they are able to function as a mutually supportive team of people;
- the extent to which your people believe they are engaged in valuable work; and
- the expectations you have of your people and your ability to provide them with appropriate rewards and recognition.

If you want to know what motivates your people, ask them, because making an assumption about the things that increase their interest in their work can be counter-productive.

A study undertaken by Kenneth Korvacs[10] some years ago asked a large number of people, across a wide spectrum of industries, what motivated them most: salary, job security, personal interest, interesting job, appreciation, involvement, promotion and growth, working conditions, loyalty and tactful discipline. The study also surveyed their managers and supervisors, who rated salary, job security, and promotion and growth as the top three motivators.

The three most popular among the staff surveyed were:

- appreciation
- involvement
- personal interest

The point to be aware of in these survey results is that the managers rated 'appreciation', 'involvement', and 'personal interest' as the *least* important motivators of their staff.

Times and circumstances have changed. It may be that other things are more important for your people. You will not know unless you ask them. Do this in such a way that you are sure that you are being given honest answers.

Continuing research tells us that the most important aspects of motivating your staff are personal interest, involvement, appreciation or recognition, and the expectation you have of them. The most critical of these are the last two—recognition and expectation.

In showing a personal interest care should be taken not to invade a colleague's privacy. Creating open communication with your team builds trust, leading to more spontaneous communication on non-work issues. This means knowing about them as people not just as workers, knowing what motivates them as individuals. It means knowing what is important for them at work and in their lives outside work. It means knowing how their outside interests affect their work commitments and how they might be optimised without compromising fundamental work objectives. It means knowing what compromises are useful at a time of stress.

Personal interest is a two-way street. The extent to which you can be seen to be a real person with real issues, in the work place and elsewhere, will contribute strongly to a motivational environment for you and your team. Involvement is even more important. This has implications for the way you relate to your team both as a team and as individuals.

At the team level there are great advantages in involving everyone in the general or overall direction of the team. There are similar benefits in involving your team in the direction of the department to which your team belongs, or, for that matter, the whole organisation.

At the individual level, involvement is equally important. When you give a task to someone, it is useful to involve them in the full context of the particular task. This means discussing context, value and the ultimate purpose of the task. Without a close involvement at the task level, a team member may not be able to properly decide what is relevant in the many different situations which may arise. Nor will they know how the task fits into a broader picture for you and the team. They may not know to what standard to complete the work, or how much time to spend on it or the relative value of the client.

When team members are properly involved in their work; the effort put into motivating them is repaid.

BUILDING HIGH PERFORMANCE
PEOPLE—EXPECTATIONS

Performance improvement through high positive expectations is exponential. This is because the expectations you have of your people is one of the key motivating forces available to you.

The value of expectations in personal performance was pioneered by psychologist Robert Rosenthall in the 1970s. Since then, experiments throughout the world have supported the enormous potential of using positive expectations in performance improvement. Rosenthall conducted a number of experiments; essentially, randomly chosen schoolchildren were allotted randomly selected teachers. The teachers were told that the children were the brightest and most intelligent in their school district. The teachers were also told that they were the most gifted teachers in the school district. Within a a few months the students were out-performing their peers throughout the school district by some 20 per cent.

Another experiment involved telling a teacher that a small number of (randomly selected) children in a single class were the most intelligent in the class. Again they out performed their peers radically. The reason seems clear. By word, intonation and gesture, the students picked up a clear message. 'Mistakes', for example, were seen as aberrations from an expected high standard. Achievement at a high standard was seen as normal. In this environment it was almost impossible for the children not to be 'motivated' to very high performance levels. They were responding to the high expectations of their teachers.

Other students in the class adopt the same level of expectation, although it is differently and more subtly expressed. Students in classes of the homogenously super-bright build their own mutual support system based on the high expectations of their teacher.

A perfect illustration of the effect of high expectations is the true story about performance improvement as told in the film *Stand and Deliver*.[11] A teacher at Garfield High in East Los Angeles took a group of eighteen down-and-out Spanish-American children to college entrance standard in advanced calculus. A college entrance standard pass was unheard of in the 28-year history of the school which was in danger of losing its accreditation. Other schools in the district were lucky to have one or two students reach this standard. When all eighteen students passed, some at maximum level, there were charges of cheating. The grades were restored after the eighteen resat the examination on one day's

81

notice. Five years later 87 students from the same school passed college level calculus.

It was tough, demanding work on the part of the teacher and it was done through high positive expectations, individually and collectively, coupled with strong bonding in the classroom. The teacher's conversation was liberally sprinkled with such phrases as: 'You are the best', 'You are the champions', 'I know you can do it', 'You are not going to let this beat you'.

The work of Margaret Collins in building performance in high school students in ghetto Chicago is equally remarkable. Collins left the Chicago school system to set up her own school for street kids. Using high positive expectations and a tough, supporting environment she improved their performance from regular 'fail' grades to A and A+ grades in three months.

Expectations come from a number of major sources in our lives. First and very significant are our parents'. Second, are those we place on ourselves. And, finally, there are the expectations we receive from other key people in our lives: close personal friends at school, at work and at play; school teachers; and employers.

When the pattern of expectation is constant and fuelled by genuine feedback and recognition, performance follows expectation almost miraculously. I recall my mother saying constantly from my late teens when I first began to drive a car: 'Peter's so lucky. He always finds a parking space right outside the shop [or theatre or restaurant]—it doesn't seem to matter how busy the traffic is.' I never understood where this expectation came from. It was repeated to me, and to my friends and acquaintances in my hearing, time and time again. Thirty years or so later I still have no difficulty in finding a parking spot—in my home town, interstate or overseas. My mother's early expectation of me is now very much my own.

It always works and does so in every aspect of life where strong positive expectations are provided.

Try using: 'What a great job. Just the sort of work I expect from a person with your natural ability. You sure have a great future in this organisation.' Or 'I'm giving this task to you because, although it's quite complex and difficult, you've all the skill necessary to do a great job. Let me know if you need any assistance.' Or 'Come on! You're too good to turn in work like that. That's not your kind of work. I know you can do better. Why not do it again to your usual high standard. You know, I use your work as a model for the whole team!' Unfortunately, this is not how it is in many environments. 'There you go again. I just knew I couldn't rely on you to do it without checking on you every moment of the day. It serves me right for giving it to you to do!'

In many instances, the negative expectations are unspoken. Examples of this include: a failure to repeat a trust; delegating a task to someone else without saying why; giving a person different responsibilities; placing too tight a restriction on an associate and 'hovering' over an associate with a deadline to meet. These are all examples of unspoken negative expectations.

In this context 'Trust' is an interesting phenomenon in our relations with others. It normally means: 'I will trust you until you violate my trust and then you are untrustworthy'. It should mean, 'I trust you. I know you will always do your utmost to maintain my trust. If you happen to violate my trust I am certain this was because of the difficult circumstances you operated in at the time. My trust in you is as strong as ever. You are trustworthy'. The first attitude about trust holds a strong negative expectation. You can almost sense its owner looking for a violation to justify the negative expectation. The second attitude holds a strong positive expectation.

People perform according to the dominant expectation they have at a particular performance level. You will find your constant negative subliminal messages confirm your worst fears—your team are poor performers, hardly worth their pay. This puts your team, and yourself, on a self-perpetuating downward spiral of beautifully reinforced negative expectations.

Think about it. Your parents called you an untidy so-and-so and told you to go back to your room and tidy it all up and not to return until you had done so, even if it took forever. Even when you had your room tidy, your self-image as an *untidy person*, based on the constant reinforcement of your parents' negative expectation of you, drove you very quickly to creating its realisation. You rendered your room untidy very creatively and very quickly. Think how differently you might have behaved had the message been: 'You're too good for that kind of performance. You're better than that. I know you are tidy in everything else you do. Why don't you make sure that your room matches the way you really are.' If you have teenage children, try it. Suspend judgement on the likely results and *behave* for a month or two as if your spoken expectation was real for you and watch the positive changes occur.

Your choice as a leader, as a person who works with other people, and who wants to encourage top performance around you, is clear. Increase your expectations of your colleagues and watch with pride as they lift their performance towards their full potential. The higher the expectation the better. Why not be the leader who really challenges your people to out-perform their wildest dreams? Too many managers fail to challenge or extend their people. They put up with a second-rate performance.

The expectation I have of you as a reader of this book is that you will use high positive expectations with your colleagues. You are too good to allow yourself to be held back by limiting another's performance. You are the kind of person who likes to develop others and you thrive on seeing people around you develop.

BUILDING HIGH PERFORMANCE PEOPLE—RECOGNITION

Recognition through feedback and reward systems is the second principal aspect of building high performance people. It provides an environment in which your people are motivated to higher and higher levels of performance. This is important, as each of us, as normal functioning or rational[12] human beings, has a deeply felt desire or wish for appreciation and recognition. An entirely rational person does not *depend* on recognition. If we are not entirely rational in our psychological make-up, a desire for recognition becomes a need for appreciation and recognition.

Whatever the case, you as a leader of a team of people can fulfil a critical function when you fully recognise the achievements of your people. Recognition reinforces what the rational person knows is effective behaviour. The more recognition we get, the more likely we are to repeat the activity that prompted it. If an act is unrecognised, the individual concerned is immediately thrown back onto their own internal recognition system. When there is a dependency on recognition, the internal measure is not enough and the absence of external recognition causes doubt and uncertainty. There is a likelihood of risk aversion, and a self-limiting pattern of behaviour may develop.

In areas in which you are extending your people, where there is an element of uncertainty, there is no internal measure of satisfactory performance, even for the rational person. Your recognition is needed to guide them in developing that inner measure of their own value in the new task.

Moving into unchartered waters is even more difficult for

84

people with a dependency on recognition. Giving them recognition is akin to working in a bottomless pit. Nonetheless, as the team leader and supporter, you will find it useful to meet their needs for as long as it takes to establish an acceptable degree of internal strength. For one particular task, at least, a dependency may be reduced to a, healthier, desire for recognition.

My experience is that most people find it difficult to publicly acknowledge that they want recognition or appreciation. In private it will be their first comment about their work. This is strikingly obvious in all my consulting work. Even in organisations which are commonly regarded as top performers in their field, the desire for recognition and appreciation is strong. The absence of recognition is the most common complaint about the way an organisation is run.

In my seminars I talk of the desire we all have for recognition. I suggest that for most of us it is so strong that we are all able to remember things of value we completed to a high level of performance. We remember quite strongly that 'no one noticed' and that we received no recognition. Sometimes I suggest a standing ovation when a person or group of people volunteers for an 'experiment' of one kind or another. Embarrassment quickly turns to real pleasure for the recipients. I always ask how the audience feel when giving a standing ovation, and invariably the response is positive. Occasionally I ask for volunteers who would like a standing ovation without having to say why they want one. The reaction is the same. The recipient beams with real pleasure, and so do the donors. Every one wins!

There are two areas in which this phenomenon can have a direct effect on your own behaviour and on the way you relate to your team. First, there is your relationship with the individuals in your team in an ongoing way, day-to-day. Second, there is the extent to which you can institutionalise recognition and rewards in your team environment. The first is a prerequisite for the second. Much of the point of institutionalised recognition and reward systems is lost if the personal day-to-day feedback is missing or mainly negative.

Recognition through personal feedback

Most of us grew up in or now work in what Ken Blanchard[13] calls the 'Leave-alone-ZAP!' school of management. Let me give you a personal example. A few years ago I was intent on becoming a top radio personality. Many years earlier I had been introduced to a famous British actor. As he shook my hand and acknowledged me by name, he followed with 'What a wonderful voice. You should be on radio'. More than 20 years later his expectation was still with me. So I had the voice and I had discovered a vehicle for my goal in a very professional local community radio station. I improved my technique and delivery to the point where I was 'near commercial'. I needed feedback from people whose judgement I valued—in particular, the station manager. To my request for feedback, he replied: 'Good God, Peter, I've been in this business for more than 20 years and work on the basis that if no one says anything to me I assume everything is fine'.

It may have worked for him. In this particular situation, it didn't work for me. I wanted feedback of a detailed kind: where could I improve? What was working well for me? How could I build on my strengths? What were the areas of weakness on which I could practise and what should I avoid?

My station manager worked on the 'Leave-alone–ZAP' principle. Nothing was said until something went wrong and then the whole world knew about it. Personal feedback therefore comes in two general forms. First there is the positive reinforcement of the behaviour you want to encourage. The second is corrective feedback, driving performance forward to the desired behaviour. Both are expressed positively. There is no place in good feedback for dwelling on what you do not want or on negative behaviour.

Always focus on positive reinforcement and refer to your high positive expectations. Let your team know how highly you regard them and be specific about the behaviour that you are reinforcing. In giving corrective feedback always refer to the behaviour, not the person. Go out of your way to discover what your people are doing well and reinforce that behaviour. Do not spend your time looking for behaviour at a lesser standard than expected. When such behaviour is brought to your attention, deal with it directly by referring back to your positive expectation of them.

The four characteristics of good feedback are:

- personal,
- immediate,
- specific and
- unexpected.

To ask someone else to give feedback is the big 'no' of effective feedback. Whatever the justification, the real message you give is that you do not care. If you cannot make the direct personal contact at the time, drop a note to the person concerned. I have had a personal card printed with the message: 'Thank you! You've really done a great job! I sincerely appreciate the effort you've taken on my behalf.' I use this to reflect my pleasure in receiving outstanding customer service.

Immediacy speaks for itself. If feedback is given on the spot, the recipient knows exactly what behaviour is being addressed. If it is delayed, the behaviour you wish to support may be diminished.

Good feedback is specific to the event. A general statement about good behaviour has far less effect than a specific comment. I once had the pleasure of sitting in on an appraisal interview in which the supervising manager was an absolute expert at this. Whenever we dealt with the general characteristic, she always referred back to two or three quite specific instances. You could feel the pride of the interviewee on hearing the recognition. It was clearly no mere palliative; there was real meaning behind the message.

Good feedback is unexpected. It is not part of a technique or routine. If you plan to 'manage by walking around', be unexpected. Look for all the good things that are happening. Notice things that are happening to schedule. Notice excellent customer service and comment on it as being the behaviour you want in your team.

Recognition through reward systems

'Institutionalised' reward systems vary from informal team-based activities to structured performance agreements.

Informal activities

Informal activities encompass a range of team activities, for example:

- regular afternoon or morning teas in which events of note are publicly recognised;
- weekly and monthly 'drinks' or luncheons can be held to provide a vehicle for public recognition of activity that supports the goals and objectives of the team or organisation. The recognition can be based on individual performance or team performance; (Be careful to support the positive behaviour of the individual; don't belittle the performance of others);
- public 'brag sessions' where you ask individuals to stand up and acknowledge their own and their team performance;

- 'success sheets' circulated among your team members. Again these are generated by individuals and team leaders so they can blow their own trumpet.

These last two practices are ideal ways of complementing your personal discovery of all the positive things that occur in your team. At first you may find people a little reluctant to acknowledge their achievements. You may have to play an active role in encouraging them and you may have to use your own knowledge about the performance of your team to 'seed' the practice.

When putting informal procedures into place, it would make good sense to ask your team how best to make their performance more public. Ask them what they want and how they would like appreciation at the public level to be expressed.

Structured performance agreements

The more formal or structured recognition systems involve performance rewards and incentives. These include commission payments, bonuses and non-cash incentives such as special parking, office accommodation, increased support staff, either on a permanent or temporary basis. It includes 'person of the month' or 'person of the year' awards, dinner for two, trips interstate or overseas. Your imagination and the nature of any industrial award under which your team operates will determine what you do.

Remember that all formal reward systems must be related to supporting the kind of behaviour you wish to encourage. If you value team behaviour above individual behaviour, the rewards and recognition for team performance must obviously be more significant than those for individual performance.

Again, it is wise to involve your people in the design of reward systems. If they have participated in deciding on the goals and objectives of your team or organisation, they will be able to offer relevant advice about the most appropriate rewards, both for exceptional performance and for mutually agreed standards of performance.

Involving your people in many aspects of individual and team performance, including rewards for achievement, does not mean you have to follow their advice. Their view is very relevant and should be taken into account. As you are the leader, you take full responsibility for the decisions of the team. Be aware that participation and involvement are not the same as consensus. While both are ways of exercising your responsibility, participation and involvement imply the right of decision rests with you, the leader, and consensus implies the decision is given to the team. However, be aware in the latter instance that the competence of the team must match the complexity of the decision you ask of it.

WORKING WITH YOUR SECRETARY OR PERSONAL ASSISTANT

If you are fortunate enough to have a secretary or personal assistant, he or she may well be your most important staff resource. In no other relationship will you find the principles of involvement, high positive expectations and recognition to be of more significance.

Your personal assistant ranks with your receptionist or telephonist as the first point of contact for people outside your team or organisation. You should encourage as much mutual respect in your relationship with your assistant as possible. The relationship can be close, friendly and cooperative without becoming so personal as to affect other relationships that are important to you. Openness and integrity also play a significant, if not critical, role.

When your assistant knows your vision, your values, your goals and objectives, and what it takes to make them work, you have an invaluable resource at your disposal. The more your assistant knows about your projects, their milestones and their other critical features the better. Your effectiveness is improved when your assistant knows which clients or colleagues are significant to you.

The closer your assistant works with you and the more he or she knows about your priorities, the more likely you are to have someone who can respond intelligently to direct contact with colleagues or clients when you are unavailable. When this occurs, you have someone to whom you can delegate a significant part of your work in a meaningful and worthwhile way. You develop in the relationship a sensitivity that encourages a level of communication and expectation that has a direct effect on your performance. Your personal assistant becomes an integral member of your team.

In many work environments I have observed, there is almost a 'them' and 'us' tension in the relationship. The managers 'expect' more and do not communicate their expectations well. The personal assistants want more responsibility and want to be extended but there is no climate of trust, understanding and cooperation that will encourage this. The relationship is a waste of time and productive energies.

It is unreasonable to expect your personal assistant to make the first move in these circumstances. It is necessary for you to begin the process by establishing an atmosphere of trust and openness. This is an important responsibility of yours as leader; the performance improvement you will secure, will more than justify the effort.

The relationship you create with your personal assistant provides an underlying support that goes far beyond any dollar value. With it comes a degree of certainty about your work. You do not have to spend time being concerned about whether basic things are being done efficiently, or whether there will be problems for you when you return to the office.

Your relationship is one of mutual respect; your personal assistant is an expert in all his or her work, and you are the expert in yours. You respect the ability of your personal assistant to handle all relevant work and to advise you of any issues or concerns. You keep your personal assistant fully informed so that the work can be done on your behalf and issues of direct relevance to you are brought to your attention. Your personal assistant will know precisely in what circumstances you may be contacted when you are away from your office, or when to interrupt you in conference with an important client or colleague.

Quality performance by your assistant frees you to concentrate on work where you add value for you, your team and your organisation.

INTERVIEWS

From time to time you may find it necessary to have a more or less formal interview with one of your people. Almost certainly you will have some form of annual review or appraisal scheme.

The interview might be about a matter you have initiated, or it may be initiated by your team member in order to discuss leave or other housekeeping issues. It may be that a personal issue affecting work performance needs discussion in a more or less formal way. Whatever the basis of the meeting, the importance you place on all your people will be reflected in your approach to it. The principles of good management practice discussed earlier are important. Plan for each interview carefully. Know beforehand why the interview is being held. Know what your expected outcomes are and what you want from your team member. Decide how the interview will support your team goals and objectives and those of your team members in building their performance. Know what outcomes your team member expects.

It is particularly important that your team member knows in advance why the interview is being held. There should be no surprises and no attempt at entrapment. Even an interview where the intent is wholly benign carries uncertainty with it if the person does not know why he or she has been called to an interview. It is in your own best interests for your team member to be properly prepared as far as is practicable. After all, it is, part of building a cooperative supportive atmosphere, even when something tough has to be said.

I recall on one occasion wanting to offer some special thanks to a member of my team. I walked to her work place to find her temporarily absent. I carefully asked her neighbour to tell me when my colleague was back at her work place. Fifteen minutes later she arrived panting at my office door. I made my pretty speech and she smiled with a big sigh saying: 'Is that what you wanted! I thought you were going to fire me!' She had just joined the organisation and was very concerned about 'making the grade'. My communication with her was much more complete after that.

Once you have set a time and place for your interview, be sure to maintain your commitment to it. If you do not, you may give your team member an impression that the interview is not important. It is important to you and you should convey that clearly by your commitment to the time you have set aside for it. Be prompt, be clear and be relevant. Show that you are fully prepared. If it is about salary, show that you know the relevant salary structures and where your team member sits on that structure. If it is about conditions, know what the parameters of those conditions are and the validity of any likely response you might make. If it is about performance, know exactly what you want to say.

If you have to postpone your interview, make sure that you communicate the nature of the problem to your team member so that he or she can fully understand the postponement. Then make another appointment you are certain you can meet.

Do not be hurried, or impatient to conclude the interview. Be firm about the time you have committed to it, and, by all means, be interested, fair and considerate.

Make a note at the interview of any commitments made on either side. Be clear about deadlines for any actions. Enter your own commitments in your diary or re-submission systems. Make sure you meet them or that any changes to them are communicated to and agreed upon with your team member. Enter any follow-up dates and times for the commitments that have been agreed upon by your team member in your diary. Follow them up.

All these actions show the value you place on the interview and its outcomes, and on the team member.

PERFORMANCE APPRAISALS

Performance appraisals are a special kind of interview and feedback mechanism. After a lot of experience in designing and operating appraisals, I find I am more ambivalent about them than ever before. Very few of them work, or at least, work as well as they were intended to work.

My attitude stems from my belief that the best form of appraisal system is the one that occurs in an ongoing way, when you recognise good performance and praise it and correct poor performance on a day-to-day basis. After all, you would not think much of an airconditioning system that monitored air temperature once a year. At their worst, appraisal systems are a (poor) fail-safe mechanism when no ongoing feedback is given. At their best, they are part of the statement of objectives against which expectation and recognition is provided from day to day.

A properly designed appraisal system contains three principal elements.[14] First there is the statement of the individual's performance objectives. This describes the outcomes expected of the team member, and how they are measured, and when they are to be completed. Second there is a statement of any specific support to be provided by the team leader in order for the team member to reach the agreed objectives. This describes the special skills with which the team leader can assist, and what training is required. There may be additional resources required and these should be specified with a delivery date. Third there is the appraisal interview itself. This has a number of functions. Basically it is a review of performance, *in an overall way*, against the previously agreed outcomes. Discuss whether commitments about support were met and how this affected performance. The primary focus of the interview, however, should be on the future. Discuss your team member's career development goals and objectives and how they should be expressed. Discuss how you can support these goals and agree on specific performance objectives. Amend the individual performance expectation agreement to reflect current team objectives in a way that supports the career goals of the team member.

Some more points about appraisal schemes are as follows:

- Performance appraisal is your responsibility, not the personnel department's, although seek their advice by all means.
- Tailor your appraisal scheme to suit each work situation rather than force an inappropriate scheme or form on employees.
- Closely involve your staff in the development of the scheme and its continual review.
- Do not start a scheme unless you are clear about what you want to achieve and are prepared to put a great amount of energy into its successful operation.

After the appraisal interview, there is the continual day-by-day reinforcement of the expectations set for each team member through recognition and rewards. This is the most important aspect of your relationship with your team; it should be your main focus with them.

CONCLUSION

Building a high performance team is about building high performance people and having them 'own' the team vision, values, goals and objectives through consultation and participation. When your team members properly own their outcomes in this way, there is a commitment to joint cooperative activity—there is a commitment to support one another in achieving those objectives, to mutual trust and understanding and to high performance.

Your role as a team leader is one of enormous challenge. It is time-consuming and infinitely rewarding. The challenge is to lift the performance of your team, individually and collectively, to levels of performance of which they may not have dreamed.

Your role is one of vision and imagination.

KEY MESSAGES FROM CHAPTER 5

- *Remember that there is no substitute for strong open communication between colleagues in any work environment. It is the basis of the trust which underpins good working relationships.*

- *You have a responsibility as a leader to be aware of the motivational environment of your colleagues, to know them individually as people and not just as colleagues. You have a responsiblity to work at honouring them for their potential, their individual skills and the contribution they make to their team.*

- *Work with your colleagues on the basis of your high positive expectations of them and their performance. Refuse to take second best. Do this without carping criticism and demeaning innuendo. Do it with strong reinforcement of their achievements and personal commitment.*

- *Set aside time to recognise good performance wherever you see it, not just at work; do it at home, in social and community groups, and at play. Go out of your way to discover people doing things well. Comment on adverse performance only when it is obvious and affects you directly.*

- *Invest in designing rewards and recognition systems, monetary and non-monetary, which support the values and objectives of your team. Do this in consultation with your colleagues.*

- *Develop a strong supportive relationship with your secretary or personal assistant. Base the relationship on total trust, and significantly extend your assistant by completely involving him or her in all your business strategies.*

- *Know that appraisal systems are no substitute for ongoing feedback based on high positive expectations. Invest carefully in the design of any appraisal system and take even more care in its effective implementation. Ensure that it focuses on future development.*

- *The people in your team are more than a 'resource': they are ultimately the basis of your success. Treat them accordingly.*

SECTION 2

Understanding change in self and others

CHAPTER 6

The nature of change

*In spite of illness, in spite of the arch-enemy
sorrow, one can remain alive long past the usual
date of disintegration if one is unafraid of
change, insatiable in intellectual curiosity,
interested in big things, and happy in small ways.*

Edith Wharton (1862–1937)

*The universe is change; our life is what our
thoughts make it.*

Marcus Aurelius Antonius (121–180 AD).

The question is not one of change itself, nor necessarily one of
the degree or speed of change. It is a question of our own personal
reaction to change. Change, after all, is constantly with us. It is a
fact of life. Each moment we experience has the effect of changing
us in some way or other that is often quite unknown to us.

If we resist change, develop rigid attitudes towards it, and
base our behaviour on the notion that there is a 'right' way for
our external world to be in order for us to be happy and productive, the stress we bring on ourselves is more than considerable—it
is downright dysfunctional. It destroys or undermines productive
capacity and the meaning of what we are trying to achieve. It
limits our ability to adjust and adapt to changing circumstances.

When we develop strategies for distinguishing between the
relevant and important expectations of change from the trivial
and unimportant ones, and when we embrace the notion that
change is an integral part of our lives, we become used to the
idea of change as challenge rather than stress.[1] We are more
psychologically open, more productive and significantly more
motivated.

97

In short, those of us who have a positive attitude towards change welcome it for the opportunity and excitement it brings to our lives. Those of us who resist change do so at the cost of reduced achievement and increased stress. Your full potential, both as an individual and as a leader of your team or organisation, is directly related to your capacity to change. This relates to the techniques of personal productivity that follow in section 3 as much as to those substantive leadership issues addressed in earlier chapters.

The importance of an individual's attitude to change and the difficulty many of us have in dealing with change, even when we know it is 'for our good', is recognised throughout this book. In a number of instances tips and techniques are provided to assist you. My purpose in this chapter is to explore the difference between an open and expansive view of the personal change process and a view that is reactive and defensive. I shall examine how we deal with change and suggest ways of improving our attitude towards it.

> *People are always blaming their circumstances for*
> *what they are. I don't believe in circumstances.*
> *The people who get on in this world are the*
> *people who get up and look for the circumstances*
> *they want, and, if they can't find them,*
> *make them.*

George Bernard Shaw (1856–1950)

THE NATURE OF THE PERSONAL CHANGE PROCESS

My experience tells me that in a myriad different aspects of our lives, we build patterns of belief about the way the world is for us. These beliefs tell us how to respond emotionally and behaviourally, how we feel about a particular event and what we do about it.

A belief begins as a conscious interpretation of what that event meant for us in all its ramifications. The belief causes an emotional reaction. This in turn may be followed by a discernible behavioural response. When the event is repeated we tap into our previous experience and reinforce our belief about what that particular

98

event meant. Over time the belief becomes embedded in our subconscious minds. This belief then triggers an identical emotional and/or behavioural response each time we experience the event or set of circumstances, *or any similar event or set of circumstances to which our initial interpretations apply.* Our conscious minds record the observation of the event, and the emotional and behavioural response triggered by the subconscious belief.

Our inability to articulate the belief (the meaning of an event) that prompts an emotional and/or behavioural response, or to bring it to our conscious minds, and the speed with which it directs our responses, *leads to the quite erroneous belief that the event was the cause of the response.* Say, for example, when I was about twelve months old, I was displayed by my parents, with great love and pride, to numbers of their friends. The first time this happened I may have interpreted the event (my introduction to a complete stranger) in this way: 'Gee, who is this person? He/she looks quite different from the two people I know so well. He/she is making such strange noises. He/she is probably going to harm me in some way that I will not like.' I then feel an emotional response called fear, followed by a behavioural response called crying. Both of my reactions are entirely rational, based on my interpretation of the event.

My initial belief in a threat to my personal security may be reinforced if I am then picked up by this stranger and taken away from my mother even for a short period of time. This may be diminished by an experienced 'baby-person' who builds a rapport with me and in other ways supports a view contrary to my initial belief. If the initial event relates to two, three or four people at a time, my fear is likely to be potentiated and my crying that much more intense and heart-felt.

The next time this happens—and it happens a lot, and regularly, every time my mother goes shopping, visits her friends, plays tennis or visits the school where my father works—I shall remember my initial belief, the level of emotional and behavioural response it caused, and I shall respond accordingly. Each time it happens I may modify my belief slightly, *although my strong inclination is to adhere to my initial belief and to justify it to myself.*

As a young child I might, as a result, go to considerable lengths to avoid company in my parents' home, or I might be the most gregarious of children. As an adult I might maintain a shyness and shun public-speaking appearances, or I might welcome the opportunities I have to meet new people and speak in public about those things that are important to me. My predilection will depend initially on the belief I have about those events and the degree to which I have generalised it from my earliest experiences.

Similarly, as a very young child, whenever I injure myself I seem to get a lot of love and attention. I may thus develop a subconscious belief that pain and love are connected. Depending on whether I believe that my parents are giving me all the love and attention I really want, I may develop this belief so firmly in my mind that I became accident-prone. I may even develop a pattern of self-destructive activity in order to receive love and attention from those people who are important to me. Or I may develop a history of hypochondria or chronic sickness in order to attract the love and attention I need.

Tom Miller, in his book *The Unfair Advantage*[2], draws a very useful analogy for the process we go through in developing our subconscious patterns of belief. He likens it to the relationship between a horse and a rider. The horse is the subconscious mind, that part of us that stores the beliefs and interpretations we have made of the various events of our life. The rider is the conscious mind analysing, deciding and consciously interpreting our reactions to the multitude of events and circumstances we experience. The role of our horse, says Dr Miller, is to keep us doing things for the rest of our lives in the same way we have previously done them. The horse interprets 'different' or 'new' as 'wrong' and drives us back to doing things the way we have always done them.

> *Faced with the choice between changing one's*
> *mind and proving there is no need to do so,*
> *almost everyone gets busy on the proof.*

> John Kenneth Galbraith (1908–)

Our rider decides to give up smoking, to take more regular exercise, to go on a new diet, or to adopt a different behavioural style in relation to our colleagues. Our horse sees to it that the process of making and maintaining those changes is difficult, if not impossible. Our horse almost always wins! Tom Miller describes the process of learning to drive a motor vehicle in order to reinforce the point of his analogy. When we took our first driving lesson, our conscious attention (rider) was very much in evidence. We followed a set of instructions from book and instruc-

tor very closely: key—ignition—start-up—gear—clutch—brake—
rear vision—steering wheel—road, etc. And we were lucky if we
didn't make quite a mess of it at first. After a short while, still
with our conscious attention very much to the fore, we became
more comfortable with coordinating the multiplicity of functions
we had to perform in order to drive the vehicle with any degree
of competence.

There are many times when we drive to work or to a friend's
home when we are barely conscious of having driven there. It's
as if the car were being driven by an automatic pilot. And yet, if
we were elsewhere in the world and had to drive 'on the wrong
side of the road', our conscious attention would have to rise
considerably when negotiating our way.

When we are asked to make a change in our behaviour we
consciously or subconsciously experience an emotional response,
which in turn governs our subsequent behavioural response. This
emotional response is based directly upon our belief on what the
change means, not on the change itself which is always of neutral
value. The belief we hold about the meaning of the change
governs our emotional and behavioural reaction to the change.
This is so whether the change is 'forced' on us by the computerisa-
tion of a work procedure, a new piece of information that directly
affects the work we do, a new imperative from the CEO, or a
retrenchment. What we do emotionally and behaviourally about
the change is based solely on our subconscious understanding
about what the change means.

Understanding that we are directly and *personally* responsible
for our reaction to change is the key to managing resistance to
change and to fostering our willingness to embrace change as a
challenge rather than as a catastrophe.

Every time we are asked to make a behavioural or attitudinal
change, it means changing a belief about what the change means.
This belief is almost always responsible for an emotional response
called discomfort, anxiety, fear or even anger. The discomfort
derives from doing something new and different. Anxiety and fear
may derive from anticipation of the uncertainty of casting away
existing and comfortable behaviour in specific areas. Frustration
and anger may be extensions of the (subconsciously perceived)
threat to our very existence.

In my seminars I often introduce the notion of change with
an exercise. The group is asked to pair off. Each pair stands about
a metre apart and is asked to 'observe' the other person, noticing
everything there is to see about their partner, and to witness their

own thoughts as they do so. Then each person is asked to face away from their partner and 'make five changes to their appearance'. There is a lot of embarrassed laughter and a great hubbub of noise as they begin to explore what changes they can make: removing earrings, changing a watch from one wrist to another, loosening a belt or a tie, changing a hairstyle, undoing a collar, removing a shoe or sock or rolling up a sleeve or trouser leg. When this has been done, they are asked to face their partner again and 'to identify the changes'. This causes a lot more hilarity and not an inconsiderable amount of quite ribald commentary. Next they are asked to turn away from their partner and 'make five more changes'. Further laughter and protest ensues and once this has been done they face their partner and identify the changes once more. By this time the energy in the room is very high. Often some quite outrageous 'changes' have now occurred.

We then discuss the process. I listen to their comments and ask about what they thought at each stage of the exercise, what their reactions were and how they felt about them. The discussion of course varies widely, depending on the number of people undertaking the exercise, their ages and their backgrounds.

Within minutes of the discussion beginning, and without any instruction from me, the participants 'change' back to the physical state they were in when the exercise began. This is how strong is the need to maintain the status quo, particularly in circumstances of potential embarrassment!

Another simple exercise I sometimes use is to ask participants to clasp their hands with fingers interlocked. We then notice how many have their right thumb on top and how many have the left thumb on top. I then ask each participant to unclasp their hands and re-clasp them so that the other thumb is on top.

The ensuing conversation is interesting. They speak of their previous lack of awareness of the simple act of clasping their hands. More particularly they speak of the discomfort they feel at doing something differently from the way they have always done it.

Some things we want to change seem to take no conscious effort, others are more difficult if not 'impossible'. Change is rarely impossible. It is always a question of the amount of energy you use to address it, together with its importance to you. I gave up smoking cold turkey in 1971 and have never had the desire to smoke since. Indeed, in the past ten years or so I have become quite intolerant of other people smoking in my vicinity. Other changes of equal importance and significance I have tried to make are still on the 'wish list' after many years.

And so it is for most of us. Some changes are easy to make, despite the (subconscious) discomfort and fear we experience. Sometimes we are able to tap into an inner resource that makes the change happen without a lot of conscious attention to the process. Other changes we know are good for us are still to be made or have been long since forgotten.

When you are making a personal change, there is a direct relationship between your desire for a change and the person making the change! When you want to bring about change in others, work colleagues, family, social groups and neighbourhoods, there is a much more complex set of relationships to manage. The principles of the change process in individuals apply equally to the individuals of teams and to large organisations. After all it is the people of the team who will together create the change in the team behaviour and performance. The next two chapters explore the process required for effectively creating change in yourself and others.

KEY MESSAGES FROM CHAPTER 6

- *Become more aware of the way people who are close to you respond to change; listen to how well they accept personal responsibility for their emotional response.*

- *Be aware of your emotional and behavioural responses to change, about how you respond to external requests and suggestions for change. Notice any defensiveness you experience. Notice who and what you 'blame' for your response.*

- *Try asking yourself, when you explore your emotional and behavioural responses, what belief you have which might have caused yourself to respond in that way.*

CHAPTER 7

Leading change in self

There are two key elements in eliminating old behaviour in favour of a new preferred one. The first of these is the extent to which you can draw on an emotional commitment to the change you wish to make. The second is your ability to deal with the rational and irrational beliefs which underpin the emotional response you experience when change is wanted. This involves a desire to release the previous behaviour coupled with a desire to embrace the new. And of course there is a need to practice the new behaviour until it becomes 'second nature'.

COMMITMENT TO CHANGE

We have seen in the previous chapter that it is critical to maintain conscious attention on any change you are about to make. This means that, if the change is important to you, there is a good chance the change can be readily effected. It also means that, if the change 'seemed like a good thing at the time', or was wished on you by someone else and does not tap into your own sense of priorities, it is not likely to occur. It further means that, if there are a number of things you want to implement at one time, there is less likely to be effective action. This is simply because too little attention is given to each item, certainly not enough to override the intensity with which the subconscious holds onto past beliefs and the discomfort this brings. Of course, when all the changes relate to one overall pattern of change in one direction, and this is important to you, there is a much stronger likelihood of success.

It is therefore important that you have a strong sense of purpose and know what your core values are. Once these are clear to you, it is much easier to devote the time and attention to making change work.

I vividly recall a television interview with a swimmer who had won a gold medal in the 400 metres breast-stroke event at the 1990 Commonwealth Games in Auckland. He said: 'Ever since Edinburgh [the venue of the previous Commonwealth Games], all I could see was the gold medal at the end of the pool'. Think how easy it would be for you to take decisions and make changes to patterns of behaviour if that were the intensity of your focus and commitment to the outcome you wanted. Improved diet and changes to exercise and training regimes and sleeping habits would all fall into place quite 'naturally'.

The extent to which you hold a strong picture of the direction of your life, the extent to which you are 'on purpose', and have the will to make the changes you wish, to serve the overall goal you have for yourself, will largely determine your capacity to devote time and energy to making the change work for you. Without these things it is extremely likely that there will be some intervening imperative that will take your attention away from the change. Your subconscious self will drive you back to where you previously felt comfortable. This is why it is important to have a strong commitment to your own lifetime goals and the major goals you want to achieve in order to render those lifetime goals meaningful for you. Every fibre of your conscious mind should become directed towards the purpose you have set yourself. The changes you want to make will become easy to identify and implement.

If you find it difficult to develop a sense of lifetime purpose, even after following the suggestions I make earlier in this book, do not despair. Read and research those areas of endeavour that do interest you. Gather experiences and create a network of relationships in the general area. Sooner or later your 'purpose' will fall into place for you.

My experience is relevant here. For many years I had a general idea of where I wanted to go and what my purpose was. I knew it was not in the area of the techniques of management, the various formulas of the management 'fads' of the day. They all seemed too transient and ephemeral; they worked to a degree in some parts of some organisations and not in others. They seemed to be forgotten soon after they were implemented.

Increasingly my experience led me to the view that the people in the organisation made the difference, that front-line staff and their team leaders were just as important as chief executives and members of the boards of directors. Indeed, as I moved into more and more consulting work, I came to believe that the front-line staff and their team leaders were even more critical to the long-term success of the organisation than the chief executive. There are, it is true, the (rare) role models provided for us in the many texts on leadership. Ask yourself, however, how many of them have skills that survive over time or translate to other organisations *without the active engagement of the minds and bodies of their front-line staff*. It is clearly a function of a continuing relationship between the two.

As I was putting the finishing touches to this book, gaining more and more insight into the way organisations seemed to operate, I became convinced that organisational success lay ultimately in the relationships that existed among the organisation's people, and in their need to enjoy consistently high 'self-esteem' and to perceive themselves as busy, productive members of their organisation.

Organisational success also involved the existence of quality relationships between the people who made up the team or organisation, based on mutual respect and trust, each person valuing the others for their uniqueness and for their skills and qualities. It also concerned relationships between people and their organisation, and the extent of their mutual contribution to shared values and to the direction of the organisation and the work conditions of the organisation.

It became clear to me that many of the catchphrases of the day—customer service, total quality management and service, the learning organisation, business process re-engineering, leadership—all depended on the continuing quality of the relationships of those who made up the organisation.

My purpose became clear: my business vision was and is to encourage and develop the radical improvement of organisations through consulting and training activity—activity designed to improve the performance of individuals, teams and organisations by developing their relationships skills. This serves my lifetime personal goal and the values I have articulated over the years. Much of my work involves taking risks with new things and new circumstances and I know it serves my business vision.

The work and the changes associated with it are readily achievable. Without this congruence, I would procrastinate and become prone to irritation and frustration. This does not mean that when I am on purpose, changes are easy, or that I feel no fear, or experience no anxiety. It merely means that my intention is strong enough to override my fear and maintain my conscious attention on getting the job done, along with the changes that are involved in the process. Quite recently I was asked to give a series of seminars for an organisation responsible for training unemployed people in new and relevant skills. One occasion involved about 25 people, half of whom were trainee welders—male, tough and uncommunicative. The remainder were computer skills trainees—female, gentle, a little uncertain and with some language difficulties. I was given two hours with the group to improve their self-esteem and give them a sense of their own power through cooperative activity and goal setting.

When I arrived, the room was poorly suited to my purpose. Males and females sat on opposite sides of the room and did not appear to want to speak to each other—they had never previously met in the college. It was far more of a challenge than I had imagined. The material and activities I had prepared were substantially new to me. What was even more of a 'stretch' was that I had chosen to dress in jeans, T-shirt and sneakers, rather than the usual corporate suit and tie.

I was clear about my purpose, however, and the work related directly to my overall business goals. I took a big breath and went for it. The result was amazing. I attended the group's graduation several weeks later and there was not one student who did not take the trouble to show his or her appreciation of the distance we had been able to travel together.

Earlier, when I was less clear about my inner direction, my fear of doing something new and different like this might well have prevented me from undertaking the work. Then I felt obliged to stay very close to the 'script' with which I was thoroughly comfortable.

Now I say 'no' to work and experiences that do not contribute to my overall vision and sense of purpose, and 'yes, thanks' to work that does. If there is a stretch involved, I take it in my stride. This does not mean I feel no fear. It means the fear is acknowledged and accepted as part of the challenge; in many cases fear gives way to excitement. Indeed, fear, it seems, is the 'flip side' of excitement. The result is always worthwhile and reinforces my growing sense of purpose in my vision. You see, it is more than just words; it is a sense of commitment and underlying purpose about everything I do. And it doesn't matter if what I know to be my vision is 'wrong' in other people's eyes. For the moment I know it is my purpose and I derive value and commitment from it. I wake up with the words singing in my mind and I look forward to my day; I go to sleep with ideas about how to create more and more opportunities in my chosen field buzzing in my head. Certainly there are some things I still shy away from, some changes I am still not prepared to make, but my sense of mission constantly reinforces my commitment to those changes I elect to make.

DEALING WITH BELIEFS ABOUT CHANGE

The common emotional response in relation to change, whether consciously experienced or not, is based on the discomfort described in the previous chapter. This is combined with an anxiety associated with anticipating something new in place of what we have previously considered satisfactory. The belief that underpins this emotional response is idiosyncratic to you and your interpretation of the events you have experienced. The extent to which that belief is relevant or rational in the present circumstances is also quite idiosyncratic to you.

The beliefs you have that prevent you from moving forward to greater levels of personal performance have been learnt. And what you have learnt can be replaced by something else. This process requires dedication and commitment. The value of the re-learning is that it is permanent. The responsibility for re-learning and changing is yours.

The process of changing the beliefs we hold about the world involves the behavioural changes necessary for improved performance. It equally involves changing the emotional or attitudinal responses we make in response to various forms of adversity in our daily lives. This can be achieved by means of a relatively formal exercise or by an informal process on a daily basis. Both involve looking closely at the underlying belief(s) in any dysfunctional situation you might experience.

A FORMAL STRUCTURE FOR MANAGING PERSONAL CHANGE

The structure I suggest is one of Martin Seligman's, based in part on the work of Albert Ellis. Tom Miller also offers a similar structure based on Albert Ellis's work. During the early 1950s Albert Ellis began to understand that to expose his patients to the reason for their fears (beliefs on which the fears were based), and to have them realise their fear was no longer appropriate, no matter how much it had been justified in previous circumstances. It was more effective to look at the reasons for behaviour than to use the conventional psychoanalytical procedures of the day. His description of his method, 'Rational Emotive Psychotherapy', appeared in a paper he presented to the annual meeting of the American Psychological Association in 1958.[1]

In the early 1960s Ellis published *Reason and Emotion in Psychotherapy*[2] in which he describes the origins of his thesis and its application to a wide range of psychoses. *A Guide to Rational Living*[3] was published in 1961 as one of the very first 'self-help' books in the field of behavioural change. This was followed in 1975 by *A New Guide to Rational Living* (written with Robert A Harper)[4] which brought Rational Emotive Therapy (RET)—a very effective method for behavioural modification—to the lay reader. Tom Miller's book *the Unfair Advantage* translates the more technical analysis of behaviour and the change process into readily understandable metaphors and exercises. He uses a similar structure for analysing inappropriate emotional response to dealing with change and making behavioural modifications. If you are interested in understanding how the structure works this book may prove more readily assimilable than Ellis's own writing.[5]

The ABC of RET is the cornerstone of a rational analysis of any dysfunctional emotional response:

- A—the event which occurred;
- B—the belief, or meaning, we give to that event; and
- C—the emotional and behavioural consequences of that belief.

The purpose of drawing on this work in this context is that it is a very effective means of dealing with 'normal', fully functional people such as ourselves in our work, family, social and community lives, whenever we experience any emotional response that inhibits higher performance. Rational Emotive Therapy is very effective in dealing with feelings of anxiety, fear, resentment, guilt and depression, not to mention sudden and unexpected frustration or anger, as well as fear of change.

Martin Seligman, a professor of psychology from the University of Pennsylvania, has devoted his own research energies to work that concludes that most, if not all, our behavioural responses have been learnt rather than acquired through heredity. His work has shown that our 'internal explanatory style' will show up as optimistic or pessimistic. Those with a highly optimistic internal explanatory style overcome adversity more readily and are significantly less prone to illness, and to conditions of anxiety or depression. Those with a predominantly pessimistic internal explanatory style tend to be the reverse—prone to bouts of transitory depression and less able to bounce back strongly from illness and temporary setbacks.

Seligman's theory is that our internal explanatory style has been learnt and can therefore be 'unlearnt' and something new and more functionally appropriate put in its place. In his book *Learned Optimism*[6], Seligman introduces a model that, drawing on Ellis's ABC, helps us to introduce new beliefs that are likely to serve us better than the old ones in those areas in which we wish to make change. Understanding this process, and the structure or model on which it is based, is a very important, if not essential, element in managing change in ourselves and in others.

CHANGING LEARNED BELIEFS AND BEHAVIOUR

Seligman's structure is a five-element one—the ABCDE of change if you like. The outline is as follows:

- Adversity
- Belief
- Consequence
- Disputation
- Energisation

The first step in his structure for relearning is to identify the Adversity. This is a neutral expression of the event or occurrence. Examples might include the following scenarios:

1 My team told me in the last round of annual appraisals that there was a need for me to provide them with more feedback in order for me to become a more effective team leader.

2 My spouse wants me to be demonstratively affectionate to her and I know this is important for the health of my family relationships.

3 On the expressway a car cuts sharply in front of me without indicating.

4 My boss told me that my application for a salary raise has been knocked back.

5 A trusted colleague told me that a long-awaited report would not be ready in time for a key meeting.

A recent experience of mine springs to mind. The Adversity (event) was the call from the telephone company I received confirming my instruction to terminate one business phone line and divert two others. It was 4.45 p.m. and I had a meeting at 6.00 p.m. I had to leave the office at 5.30. What made this event significant was that the telephone company's call was some six weeks earlier than I had instructed. The phone line on which they had called was the only line I had left. One had been disconnected and the other permanently diverted to another number.

The second step is to write down the emotional and behavioural Consequences of the event/belief sequence. This is the natural follow-on from your belief in emotional and behavioural terms. In my case, my emotional response was that I became very frustrated, then angry. In short, I 'snapped'. In behavioural terms I became quite hot and spoke to the company messenger in a way that was far less than polite and considerate. At this point I became aware of the way I was behaving and experienced feelings of 'guilt' at my behaviour, then more frustration and anger as I could not seem to control my anger and the words I was saying. I became very assertive and quite rude. The excellent skills of the telephone company messenger rescued me from my anger and the matter was resolved satisfactorily before I had to leave the office.

The third step is to describe the Belief—what underlying belief you have about the event or what possible meaning you could have given to the event itself, which would have justified the consequence. Remember, the 'belief' will be part rational and part irrational. The irrational part of the belief will be what has caused the dysfunctional emotional response. In my case frustration and irritation were justified, but anger and the tone and nature of the words used were clearly counter-productive. I was lucky the person from the telephone company was so skilled in handling 'difficult' people.

111

My personal experience and my experience in workshops and seminars indicates that describing the Belief is probably the part with which you will have most difficulty. Write down *anything* that is remotely possible just as it comes to your mind, however improbable or outrageous it seems—the more so the better.

In the example I have given of the telephone company accelerating my request for changes to my office phone system, the possible meanings I gathered went along these lines:

- This is a plot by the telephone company to damage my business.
- Someone out there wants to make me and my business look foolish—to break contact with my clients.
- The company is totally inefficient and everything it does causes damage to someone.
- The company cannot be trusted to do anything to a decent standard.
- The company is more interested in large corporations than in small businesses.
- The company knew exactly what was required and went out of its way to harm my business.

—and so on!

It is not necessary, or even desirable that the *possible* meaning you were to give to the event had to be believable in the cold hard light of day. The point of the exercise is to put down all possibilities because one such irrational belief must have been responsible for the dysfunctional behaviour.

The fourth step is the process of **Disputation**. This is an inner argument about the logic or rationality of the possible beliefs or meanings you have identified under **B**.

Seligman also writes of distraction, adoption of a thought so contrary to a belief or thought pattern about a response to an event that it completely nullifies the dysfunctional emotional response. This might take the form of imagining a hostile boss (male) dressed in a two-piece bikini delivering the usual homilies about your performance. This might well distract you from your normal fear and anger at the way you are being treated. Imagine an angry customer stark naked as you listen on the phone to their complaint and see if this does not dissipate your own adverse reaction somewhat and give you a little more space to deal with the issue in an efficient manner, untouched by an emotional reaction that might otherwise get in the way.

On the whole, Seligman prefers to dispute the beliefs rather than distract from them, and certainly this has been my experience in dealing with my own performance. Disputation means adopting one or more of the following methods of challenging the beliefs you have identified:

- What evidence do you have for your belief?
- What alternatives do you have for your belief?
- What implications are there for the belief *even if* the belief were to prove accurate?
- What is the usefulness of the belief to me? If I were to hang on to a particular belief what do I gain from doing so?

In my telephone example I concluded that there was absolutely *no evidence* that would justify my belief that the telephone company was out to damage my business. It is true that some six months previously they had failed to connect a free-call number and this had been responsible for a poor response to a series of newspaper advertisements I had run. On reflection, this hardly amounted to a deliberate conspiracy against me.

Moreover there were a number of *alternatives* to my beliefs. The telephone company was indeed well meaning and although they have since improved their performance considerably (I have direct evidence for this), there are areas in which they still need to improve. In my case they were a little over-zealous rather than incompetent. After all, they fixed the problem they created for me within half an hour while I hung onto the phone, and they couldn't have done that two or three years ago. Anyway, would running one small consultancy out of business be the way for them to win new business?

Many other alternative beliefs may occur to you as you read. If they were intent on not allowing me to operate from those premises by cutting off the phone for six weeks and by not fixing it, the *implication* could be no worse than closing the office and operating from home until the new premises became available. A quick look in my diary said that this would be inconvenient although not impossible. And the odds were that they would have been able to correct their mistake a day or two afterwards and this would be only mildly inconvenient—certainly not catastrophic!

Look at the *usefulness* of holding onto the belief. My business may have taken a nosedive at that point. I could analyse whether I was using the belief about the 'plot' to justify not changing my marketing strategy, about holding onto patterns of behaviour that I did not like. After this process I might be left with the belief that says:

The telephone company personnel are working on improving their performance. They are a bit over-zealous and thank goodness they thought to phone me anyway so that I could deal with the issue rather than discover it by default. The person who phoned me was very pleasant and effective in turning the mistake around. I was the inadvertent victim of a well-meaning error.

The fifth and final step is the process of Energisation—how you might feel if the beliefs you originally held are modified so that what you are left with is sufficiently close to the mark as to be highly probable. In my case this means I take the call from the telephone company. I am puzzled and perhaps a little annoyed. I politely explain about the commitment we had and what I need right now to have the matter sorted out to my satisfaction. I have no doubt that given the excellent manner of the person who called me, this would have resulted in very effective two-way communication. My frustration and annoyance may have remained. I would certainly not have felt any guilt at the way I conducted myself. Indeed I would have felt quietly proud of the ease with which I dealt with a potentially awkward situation.

My suggestion is that at the end of each day you identify the one event that occurred where either you were asked to behave in a new or different way, or where you did not behave as well as you might have wished. Then analyse the event using the ABCDE structure I have described. This requires application and effort. In a relatively short period of time, you will find, the changes are quite considerable. My own experience quite strongly suggests its effectiveness. I started the exercises as a result of the experience with the telephone company. I had been reading *Learned Optimism* at the time and had known through my previous reading of Ellis and Miller how intuitively sensible the process seemed, so I decided to give it a go. I did my ABCDE exercises each evening for three weeks. I started with the telephone company event and extended the exercise to personal and business events that did not work for me on the day. I did not spend a lot of time identifying the 'right' ones on which to work; there always seemed one at hand. Sometimes it was quite trivial and at other times it was a lot more serious in its longer term implications for my performance. I was interested to see how much of a theme ran through the beliefs I had on a range of events.

By three weeks I was well into the pattern of doing my ABCDE exercises, and I had another, similar, call from the telephone company still three weeks in advance of the move. At first I was incredulous. Then I reacted emotionally and behaviourally exactly as I had 'predicted' in my initial ABCDE exercise. The person who called was less skilled in difficult communication than the previous one and it was *my* skill which held the conversation on the rails. The phone system was restored within fifteen minutes.

The new responses I have learnt have translated equally effectively into other aspects of my life. I have also decided to write down two or three good things that happened to me during the day. I do this to ensure that I maintain my focus on my positive achievements each day. I now have a template document on my word processor so that I can also do my exercises in that form as the mood takes me. The process is simple enough. It is not always easy to maintain a commitment to it. Sometimes you discover some interesting things about yourself and sometimes things you would not particularly want to admit to in public.[7] There is a temptation to let the exercise go for a day or two as doing the exercise is a 'change' that is easy enough to resist.

Maintaining concentration on doing the exercises, and maintaining the momentum for improved performance by embracing change more readily, is well worthwhile.

INFORMAL PROCESSING FOR PERSONAL CHANGE

An alternative and quite simple process for analysing fear and other emotional responses involves a discursive daily diary entry. This has the advantage of being less structured, although it should always allow you to discuss in your diary what possible beliefs might have caused the emotional and behavioural response you did not like. It should also allow for a discursive disputation of those beliefs, together with a prediction of how you might behave if you had the 'ideal' for that circumstance firmly in place.

CONCLUSION

Whether you wish to make major changes of direction or not, the ability to relate flexibly to the rapidly changing environment and to rise creatively to the daily challenges this provides is the hallmark of success and achievement on a personal basis. Top performers—those who wish to lead teams of work colleagues, organisations, social or sporting groups, or families—all have this capacity to use changing circumstances to their own advantage and to make the personal changes necessary to inspire and lead.

> *If there is anything that characterises life, it is change . . . what most distinguishes the animate from the inanimate is 'irritability'. Something that's animate moves when you poke at it. It doesn't just sit there. It's alive. It goes this way and that way. It grows, it decays, it gets reborn. It changes. All life is in process.*

M Scott Peck, *A World Waiting to be Born*[8]

A further perspective on this is contained in a book by Erik Olesen[9] in which the characteristics of 'top performers' across a wide range of organisations are analysed in order to assess the qualities that enable them to handle change more effectively. The characteristics are: expect change and deal with it as a challenge; build a personal commitment and maintain focus on that commitment; be able to take control and know when to let it go; be able to bounce back from setbacks; have an optimistic attitude towards work; maintain a sense of humour; learn from any mistakes made; see 'problems' in perspective; be confident; and be willing to communicate fully and establish mutual support systems with key people.

My own experience in making lasting change in my life has led me to understand more fully the fear and the risk inherent in change. In doing so I have always been inspired by the words that follow, words I have framed on my office wall so that I maintain daily contact with their meaning for me.

> *It costs so much to be a full human being that there are very few who have the enlightenment or the courage to pay the price . . . One has to abandon altogether the search for security and reach out to the risk of living with both arms. One has to embrace the world like a lover. One has to accept pain as a condition of existence. One has to court doubt and darkness as the cost of knowing.*

Morris West, *The Shoes of the Fisherman*[10]

KEY MESSAGES FROM CHAPTER 7

- *Write down goal structures about those key areas in your life that you may wish to change. Maintain your focus through end-result imagery.*

- *We resist change when a belief we have about what an event means to us overrides our conscious desire for change.*

- *Put aside fifteen minutes daily to write the ABCDE of change for one significant event in your day that provoked a reaction you would like to change.*

- *Each day, write down three or four events that occurred to your advantage. Spend a moment congratulating yourself for your part in making it happen.*

- *Set aside a few minutes each day to write a diary note about any emotional response you had which you think you would like to improve. Explore any belief which may have given rise to your reaction.*

CHAPTER 8

Leading change in others

*All organisations are in process, but the healthier
they are the more they will be in process. The
more vibrant, the more lively they are, the more
they will be changing. And the closer to perfection
they are, the more rapidly they will be changing.*

M Scott Peck, *A World Waiting to be Born* [1]

Organisations, like individuals, face a constantly moving and
changing environment. Markets; national and international eco-
nomic and political conditions; currency fluctuations; local community standards; environmental conditions; internal dynamics;
intellectual, social and ethical considerations—these are all subject
to gentle imperceptible movement in some circumstances and
violent and sudden 'sea changes' in others. It has been said that
the only genuine predictable is change itself, even though there
are whole industries growing up around the notion that some
things are predictable.

So organisations—small or large, commercial or social all need
to adapt to external change. After all, bridges and tall buildings
are built to withstand the stresses of changing weather and environmental conditions. From time to time, organisations need to
be able to make significant changes of direction as a result of
internal imperatives. In other circumstances change is driven
externally.

This chapter is about the conditions that make it easier for an
organisation to adapt to change regardless of the source of the
change. This applies as much to large organisations as it does to
small businesses or social, community or sporting groups. It also
applies to families.

In organisations, managing change is far more complex an
exercise than it is in the individual. It is difficult enough for us

as individuals, to 'manage' our own subconscious 'horse' through a change process. In an organisation we have all the other 'horses' with all their unpredictability to take into account. This chapter is not intended to support authoritarian imperatives for change. It is not about making change occur from the top down in a 'do what I say not what I do' style of organisation, which is still all too common as we move into the new century.

It is about providing an environment in which change can and does occur 'as a way of organisational life'. Indeed its premise is that, until the environment inside the organisation is conducive to change, no decision about change, will be truly effective or lasting.

Certainly there are circumstances in which change can be forced. A receiver appointed to an organisation under threat of bankruptcy must make fairly hard-nosed decisions that involve considerable change to the organisation. If those decisions satisfactorily keep the organisation going then the changes made will have formed the basis of further change. A business owner facing a revenue shortfall, cashflow problems or a changing or declining market, should make similar hard-nosed decisions. This will itself result in substantive change in the cultural platform of the organisation, and its long-term effectiveness will only be assured if this change is taken into account. Similarly a marriage guidance counsellor called to 'fix' a marriage in which the two partners have allowed their differences to become irreconcilable has very few short-term options. The marriage will only survive in the longer term if there is a long-term commitment by both parties to maintaining the relationship, and if permanent adjustments are made to the fundamental 'culture' of the relationship as a result. Issues such as trust and openness in communication, as well as the capacity to honour differences, may need to be addressed.

My experience as a manager/leader and as a consultant in organisations of all sizes tells me quite clearly that, despite what one reads in management texts and journals, there is no formula for success when managing change. Similarly, any team or organisational leader who believes that the lessons he or she learnt from a previous organisation can be applied in the next may well be in for a surprise.

Certainly management school, management texts and journals, and our previous experiences in change processing, add value to our understanding of the way organisations work. This background acts as a signpost to managing change in your current

119

organisation or team, rather than as a precise model on how to behave under all conditions.

There are no two organisations exactly alike and the likelihood is that the subtleties of the relationships of one will be so different from the other, despite some superficial similarities, that a formula approach will fail. I have seen many examples of the formula approach and I have seen many millions of dollars spent by organisations in applying them. However attractive the short-term recommendations are, the correlation between them and the short to medium-term outcomes are normally quite minimal. The effect on the people involved, the 'ordinary' people responsible for the results in those organisations, is usually horrendous.

I have learnt that, as an external change consultant, there is a need 'to stay in the question' as long as possible. Bringing an answer to the task, prior to talking to the people involved in implementing the change, ensures that you see the information you gather almost strictly in terms of the answer you have pre-determined. This is why so many formula approaches fail. Change is therefore a long-term commitment by you as a team and organisational leader. There is a greater need, I believe, to concentrate on the environment in which the change is to occur, than on the change itself. Indeed it is true to say that if the environment is 'right', the change will be self-generating. This is a significant part of the burden of Peter Senge's landmark work[2] in which he describes eleven laws to create a 'learning organisation', in which humility and vulnerability go alongside strong visionary leadership. To be vulnerable when building organisational and team change is a major threat to most people with responsibility for the overall direction of a group of people. Often a 'leader's' vision of themselves as the fountain of all wisdom, is seriously at risk in such an environment. Their capability in the soft skills of leadership is often seriously wanting.

EMPATHIC RELATIONSHIPS . . . THE KEY ELEMENT IN A CHANGE ENVIRONMENT

Wilfred Jarvis[3] calls it 'empathic relationships'. James M Kouzes and Barry Z Posner[4] call it 'credibility'. Peter Block[5] calls it 'stewardship'. M Scott Peck[6] calls it 'community'. It is a world in which the soft skills of effective relationships are of great importance. M Scott Peck describes these skills as '. . . sense of humour and timing, . . . ability to listen, . . . courage and honesty, [and] . . . capacity for empathy'. Add to these qualities trust, respect, personal integrity and honesty and openness in communication, and you have an idea of what I mean.

Empathic relationships mean sensitivity to the hearts and minds of others. Empathy is 'our ability to understand the private world of another person, *as if* it were our own, without ever losing the "as-ifness". This [qualification] is crucial, and often difficult to maintain. When "as-ifness" disappears, *their* feelings become *our* feelings. The distortions of identification overwhelm us.'[7] In writing about empathy in the wider context of a discussion on empathy and altruism, Alfie Kohn distinguishes perspective taking, as 'the capacity to imagine the way the world looks from a vantage point other than one's own', from empathy, as 'the capacity to share in the affective life of another'.[8] He does this in the context of a notion that 'turns on a two-fold attitude toward the other [person]. On the one hand, we appreciate . . . the other's otherness; on the other hand we appreciate the humanness we have in common,' an acceptance that '. . . you are not just an object in my world but the centre of a distinct and distinctive world of your own'. There is also a difference '. . . between imagining yourself in someone else's situation and imagining *her* in her situation'.

Kouzes and Posner speak of leadership as an issue about relationships, in which the issue of credibility is the foundation. The conclusion they have made from their own research and the work of Fisher and Brown[9] is that '[b]eing able to build relationships starts by learning how to understand and see things from another's perspective.' Peter Block, author of *The Empowered Manager*,[10] writes in his new book, *Stewardship* of the need for leaders to abandon 'control' procedures in favour of building partnerships with the people responsible for results in an organisation. James A Belasco in his excellent work on change in organisations sees, *inter alia*, 'people as the key' to organisational change.[11] Similarly Stephen R Covey[12] focusses strongly on the value of empathic relationships, win/win philosophies and behaviours directed towards synergy in teams and organisations creating effective leadership.

Whatever the precise definition given by the behavioural scientists and organisational development consultants, I believe that good, effective and lasting personal relationships within an organisation form the essential platform for achievement and success. This involves the capacity to understand and honour differences in a team environment and the soft skills of trust, respect, personal integrity, and the ability to listen and to have fun.

After studying people in organisations during my long career, I have a sense of an inner tension in each of us. One part of us wants to be unique and individual. Another wants to be part of a wider group or team. Our interest in being individual is responsible for our heights of personal achievement. It is also responsible for our isolation, our interest in being 'right' no matter what the cost and even in 'proving' disadvantageous behaviour right—hence the reluctance to provide energy for change when we know the change is for the better. Personal examples here might include giving up smoking, reducing alcohol intake or increasing exercise.

Our interest in being part of a wider team gives us meaning and a sense of fulfilment. It takes us to levels of achievement often impossible to attain as individuals—design, problem solving, complex physical product, not to mention the achievement of teams in social and sporting contexts. It also means giving up part of our individuality and, sometimes, maintaining an association long past its usefulness in the interest of maintaining the bond of the team.

In moments of stress, induced perhaps by change, the individual seems to predominate. There is a tendency to recoil from real commitment to team or joint activity. There is a decrease in openness of communication and a defensiveness and negativity creeps into relationships within the team. When I work with groups of unemployed people, I find them so stressed by their position that it is very difficult for them to think about any joint activity when seeking work. There is a competitiveness and defensiveness about them that inhibits truly effective cooperation. And yet my experience is that small groups of people working in teams find employment, and much more satisfying employment, more quickly and efficiently than individuals.

In an organisation under stress [of change], there may well continue to be what M Scott Peck calls a pseudocommunity[13] in which there is a superficial civility in relationships. Tension and dissension flourish underneath, leading ultimately to a breakdown in effective communication and cooperation. Effective and lasting change is resisted and undermined even as lip-service is paid to the objectives and detail of the change. Certainly there is the antithesis of the 'learning organisation'. This applies as much to families, social and sporting groups, small and large work teams, and small businesses as it does to larger organisations.

The conditions of truly empathic relationships within an organisation, where each team member understands and honours the differences between members with love (caring), trust, respect and integrity, and can talk about those differences honestly and openly, makes any form of change much more relevant and enduring.

Differences are acknowledged and their effects taken into account. The tendency towards individual defensive behaviour which undermines effective change is diminished, if not eliminated. Indeed the pre-existence and maintenance of the qualities of empathic relationships are the essential ingredients for creating the learning organisation and the change that accompanies it.

CREATING AN ENVIRONMENT FOR CHANGE

Educare (Latin)—to lead forth from within

In my work as a consultant I have found a number of common themes regularly recurring as I discuss issues of change and direction with people in organisations. I believe they are relevant to anyone thinking about undertaking change in an organisation. Almost without fail I learn of:

- a lack of a sense of direction or purpose;
- an absence of communication within the organisation and failure to involve the front-line people in decisions that affect them; and
- failure to appreciate people for the work they do, particularly the 'extra' work above the call of duty.

It is always important for me to remember that these are the perceptions of the people with whom I talk and not necessarily the reality. Nonetheless, they lead me to a conclusion that the three key elements to effective change in an organisation are:

1 establishing empathic relationships;
2 leadership; and
3 direction and purpose.

I have isolated these three components for the sake of simplicity; they are interrelated in a complex way and should be understood in that context. Empathic relationships cannot be established under poor leadership, nor will they survive absence of direction or purpose. Direction and purpose are integral to leadership which aspires to successful and ongoing change; they are the social cement of relationships within an organisation. Change will not occur in a lasting and effective way without empathic relationships and a strong sense of direction and purpose. Establishing empathic relationships is perhaps the most important element, as it provides the wellnourished ground into which the seeds of leadership and vision can flourish.

Establishing empathic relationships

The process of establishing community or empathic relationships in an organisation is not a one-off task: it is a time-consuming and difficult undertaking. It requires continual application and commitment by all members of the organisation. As James Belasco writes, change is a continuous process and not a destination.[14] It can also be quite threatening as it requires people to relate to one another in ways that were previously not even considered in a work environment. Empathic relationships is something many people have never experienced, whether this be in family, social or sporting groups, or in the relatively formal atmosphere of corporate life. Yet this willingness to be open and vulnerable with one another is the only way true community and empathic relationships can be established. This is why the first element of the process requires the active enlistment and commitment of the leadership. This commitment must be visible, vocal and continual. Without a full commitment, there is a 'critical mass' working consciously or subconsciously against the process.

If you are a team leader in your organisation and you are fully responsible for your own results (there are no detailed 'how to' procedures in your way and within reason you are free to meet your own outcomes in your own way), you can establish empathic relationships within your own team. This will start with your declaration of your personal intent to your close colleagues, as well as their 'enrolment' in it and the processes necessary to create it. This degree of concern for a near consensual commitment of all key players in the team is essential, and demonstrates the model you wish to create. Then it is necessary to dedicate sufficient time on an ongoing basis to bringing about the desired change in relationships within your team.

A two or three-day workshop will start the process for you. A regular two to three-hour workshop every three to four weeks for three to six months followed by a one-day workshop every six months, or so will reinforce the newly developing relationship skills. The content of the workshops will embrace discussions and activities directed towards defining common outcomes for the group; mission, vision, value statements and major team outcomes. A majority of the time can be set aside for activities designed to raise discussion about personal values and personal communication styles, individual experiences and circumstances at home and at work that explain behaviours and attitudes. It will also permit resolution of individual and team issues of conflict and dispute. It should include activities and discussion that support new attitudes and behaviours of listening and understanding other people.

Needless to say, the people leading the full-day workshops must be fully qualified and experienced in the facilitation of workshops of this kind, as well as fully briefed on the background and objectives of the particular organisation. It is a role of great importance and the wellbeing of the individual and/or the team is very much in their hands.

M Scott Peck chooses to work in teams of two when facilitating what he calls 'community' workshops. This may be a good idea, offering the facilitators a balance and variety when dealing with the many issues which inevitably arise in a workshop of this nature.

Whether or not the resources you need for the workshop are available to you internally will depend on the size and sophistication of your organisation. Do not embark on the exercise unless you are fully convinced of the advantages it will bring to you and your team and unless you have the utmost confidence in the facilitators you have available for the workshop.

The importance of combining the process of relationship building with substantive (directional) team issues in the workshop is to demonstrate, as the process unfolds, the effectiveness of consensual decision making based on the new relationships you achieve in the workshop.

After the initial workshop, it is your role to model the new relationships in every aspect of the work you do. In doing so, it is worthwhile remembering that empathic relationships are not relationships in which you are expected to 'wimp out'. Empathic relationships combine a clear-headed neutral or analytical approach to the issues you and your team face, with respect, trust and integrity in the way you communicate and otherwise relate to one another.

It is just as possible to fire someone with empathy as it is to work with them empathically, coaching them to improve their performance while making short-term allowances for them as a valued colleague who has some adjustments to make.

In short, empathy is a position of strength, best summed up by the Hindu word *satyagraha*, symbolised by the elephant and meaning a unique combination of love, strength and power. *Satyagraha* was adopted by Gandhi to indicate the underlying philosophy behind his notion of passive resistance. Gandhi, in turn, inspired Martin Luther King Jnr in his work for the rights of black Americans in the 1960s.

Leadership

This has two key components. The first is the commitment to action and the second is the commitment to people. They are wholly interrelated; one is irrelevant without the other. Leaders know that people are as important as the goals they have and the actions they take in pursuit of them.

A leader's commitment to action

The commitment to action has a number of elements: a strong sense of personal vision, confidence, and willingness to take decisions. This supports another essential ingredient—a willingness to be different, to take risks. Alex Haley, the author of *Roots*, said: 'Too often we are taught how *not* to take risks. When we are children in school, for example, we are told to respect our heroes, our founders, the great people of the past. We are directed to their portraits hanging on walls and in hallways and reproduced in textbooks. What we are not told is that these leaders, who look so serene and secure in those portraits, were in fact rule-*breakers*. They were risk-takers in the best sense of the word; they dared to be different.'[15]

Without a sense of personal vision, the confidence to back it up and a strong need for action, the risks necessary to create and enlist others in effective action would be unlikely to be taken. This commitment to action involves establishing a sense of direction and underlying purpose for the people of the organisation in a way that relates directly to the particular tasks they are asked to undertake.

A leader's commitment to people

The commitment to people also has a number of key components. There is the strong interest in working towards creating empathic relationships with colleagues, customers and suppliers, involving as it does honesty and openness in communication. This is the

126

foundation of another key element called credibility. Indeed Kouzes and Posner regard this as *the* key component of leadership.[16]

This commitment to people involves providing colleagues with feedback on performance, on installing rewards and recognition systems appropriate to the mission, objectives and operating principles of the organisation. It means involving the people of the organisation in setting the organisation's direction and in the decisions flowing from it that directly relate to their sphere of activity. It involves a 'humility' in seeking opinion and advice from the people of the organisation. It is the antithesis of the omnipotent approach that has characterised much of our leadership until now. I pray that it does not endure into the new century.

All these key elements of leadership have been dealt with elsewhere in this book and, despite their significance, I shall not labour them here.

Direction and purpose

The establishment of a statement of mission or vision and of values in an organisation is one thing. The creation of direction and purpose in an organisation *in a way that the people of the organisation can relate them directly to their own jobs* is another. An excellent framework for a workshop discussion likely to draw commitment to a team mission or vision is set out in *Enlightened Leadership*[17] under 'The effective questions to develop purpose and vision'. If this cannot be done because of the sheer size or complexity of the organisation, it is essential that it be done at the divisional, department and team level, and that some opportunity exists for the leaders of smaller units to develop their own joint sense of direction and purpose.

Knowing where I am headed is a key comfort factor in my personal motivation. Knowing where my team is headed and what its precise objectives are is a key element of my motivation in my contribution to that team. An overriding sense of purpose, over and above my sense of direction, is what holds me in there when the going gets tough and the sense of direction falters however momentarily. The value of the sense of direction is not the goal or objective itself, it is the pursuit of the objective. This is the motivating force. Too strong an attachment to a specific directional statement leads to rigidity and failure to respond to new challenges and new circumstances otherwise known as change.

127

I am a member of my local volunteer bushfire brigade. When we are called out to fight a fire, my sense of 'comfort' in these dangerous circumstances derives from the clarity of definition of the objective. Once this is established I am willing to follow specific instruction and, in doing so, face whatever danger may exist. Given the circumstances, my motivation to hang in there and do my job is secure. Without a sense of direction, I become anxious and critical of what I am asked to do. My motivation is reduced and my concern becomes more personal and less concerned about the work of the team as a whole. Beyond this I have a strong sense of purpose or fulfilment in belonging to the bushfire brigade. I know that it provides an essential element of safety for many thousands of people who live on the outskirts of our cities and in our bushland. I know that it contributes to the wonderful bushland the whole community enjoys.

It is this overriding sense of purpose that keeps me wanting to continue my work in the brigade through [incredibly boring] routine meetings, the many training exercises we embark on, as well as the activity involved in fighting a house or bushfire.

CONCLUSION

Establishing empathic relationships in an organisation, providing leadership where there is a strong commitment to action and people, and creating a strong sense of direction and purpose in it, create an environment in which change will flourish. It is in these conditions that change will truly become the process, the way of life, rather than the destination.

KEY MESSAGES FROM CHAPTER 8

- *Leading change in teams is an extremely complex and time-consuming exercise. If you are not prepared to put the appropriate amount of time and energy into creating change, get out of the way and let someone else do it.*

- *Empathic relationships are the basis of effective, lasting change and of the ability to respond to change in an ongoing way.*

- *Under stress [of change] people tend to become defensive and resistant to change unless the conditions of empathic relations are in place or the organisation is recognised by the people involved as moving toward empathic relationships.*

- *Effective change requires strong leadership which involves vision, confidence and action focus, as well as a lasting commitment to empathic relationships. Effective change requires that the organisation have a sense of direction and overriding purpose to which each member of the team can relate.*

SECTION 3

Essential skills for success

CHAPTER 9

Developing your team through delegation

*Delegation is the process of hanging on tight
with an open hand . . . of sharing leadership and
developing solution-oriented people.*

Effective delegation is an essential part of leadership; it is an important element of high achievement. Delegation is not 'dumping' or merely assigning tasks. Done effectively, it is a constructive positive force in developing the people on your team.

The best way to progress and improve your productivity and performance is to delegate. Delegation is high leverage activity. What you can achieve by your own physical exertions is strictly limited. What you can achieve through developing the performance of your team members by effective delegation is almost limitless. Delegation is also an essential element of team building. It is the art and practice of sharing leadership, of developing solution rather than problem-oriented people, and of empowering your people.

DEVELOPING SOLUTION-ORIENTED PEOPLE

Attitudes towards delegation are reflected in the way we deal with the many issues or problems that arise daily in our work environment. How you react when these issues occur is a major factor in the growth and development of your team. Part of being a team leader is being asked for advice. People come to you to share a problem or concern about their work. You may see one of your team members doing something 'different', or see them struggling with a task you have delegated. Reacting positively and powerfully to these issues often means taking on the problem

133

yourself. This is a natural reaction for most of us, leading to problem-oriented, rather than *solution-oriented* team members.

Acting in a way that develops solution-oriented people has two major benefits. First it builds the confidence and achievement of individuals and develops a first-class team. Second, it frees you for even more creative work in designing new ventures, planning their implementation and developing your people even further.

Perhaps I can show you what I mean by 'solution-oriented people', by explaining what I have observed in most of the organisations with which I have worked.

A 'problem' occurs for one of the team and as soon as it is brought to the team leader's attention, the team leader launches into detailed advice on how the problem can be overcome. Often the problem is taken over completely by the team leader, especially when he or she has personal hands-on experience.

The reason this happens so frequently is a mixture of short-term expediency and ego; your reaction, as team leader, is so conditioned by experience that it seems wholly instinctive. You know exactly what is required and it is easier for you to do it; you really do not have the time to waste explaining how best to do it. Your ego is likely to be quietly flattered by all the attention it receives—an entirely subconscious reaction. Even when you feel somewhat irritated about the extra work, your ego drives you to accept it.

This is known as reverse delegation and it is a creative way to overload your work day with tasks that are really quite unimportant. It ensures that your team is dependent upon you and it trains your people to bring more and more problems to you. You are, in effect, developing problem-oriented people. Whenever they have a problem, they will bring it to you. As your problem-solving reputation becomes better known you may even find other team leaders bringing problems to you. You may find yourself volunteering for the coordination work at management team meetings.

Eventually you begin to ask yourself why you spend more and more time at work while your colleagues are at mid-week tennis or golf as part of the company's recreation and stress management program.

The trap of training problem-oriented people applies as much at home as at work. On one stress management seminar I gave, a magistrate spoke of the stress he experienced when, after taking decisions all day in court, he found that at home his wife and children came to him for help with their own work. He found this quite exhausting and very stressful; it was the last thing he wanted. I asked him what he did when his wife and children asked him to make decisions. He replied that he made the decisions and offered his advice. By doing this, he was training his family to do exactly what caused him stress.

Being free with advice and willing to solve other people's problems has more than an affect on your own performance: you are severely limiting the development of your team. When you substitute the practice of developing *solution-oriented* people, you are contributing to your own performance and to the fuller development of your team.

Begin by employing a 'what next' approach to your colleagues. This means that, instead of accepting the problem as your own or offering advice on it, you express interest, ask questions to help your colleague reach a deeper understanding of the issues, and then *ask them how they are planning to solve the problem*. In other words, put the responsibility for suggesting solutions back on their shoulders. Suggest a brainstorming session with one or two other members of the team if it is a particularly intractable problem. If you are genuinely uncertain about the outcome, join the brainstorming session and play a low-key, non-directing role. Give perspective rather than direction. Allow the solution to flow from the work of the team. This is, after all, the essential ingredient in 'double loop' communication going beyond information gathering to an understanding of the reasons and motives behind the information in a way which improves performance for you and your colleagues.[1]

When doing this be tough about dealing with the problem. Be empathetic about the way you coach your colleague through to a solution and an assessment of alternatives. Support the effort they make towards the solution. Make suggestions, or ask whether they have considered so-and-so, or how the solution proposed takes so-and-so into account.

Training solution-orientation in your team develops greater problem-solving skills and increases confidence. Soon the problems are solved without you knowing about them and the ones they do bring to you are worthy of your [joint] attention. This frees you up to focus on key high leverage activity and other issues of importance. Most importantly, you are developing your team by coaching and extending them in the most practical way possible. This builds confidence and strength and assures depth in your team.

You may find all this difficult at first. Decide in advance the minimum standards of performance to set for a task, build on them by strong communication of your expectations and by feed-back on performance, and learn to 'let go' in the process. A major challenge for leaders is to lead quietly by example and to develop solution rather than problem-oriented people. This is, after all, the key to effective delegation.

WHY WE SHOULD DELEGATE

In my seminars on leadership I often ask the group why delega-tion is necessary. As you may imagine, the answers are many and varied: the work is too menial to do myself; it is too detailed to involve me; too difficult; there is a need to ensure that things go on when I am not there; I want to build depth in my team so I can be promoted; it gives me time to think; it develops my staff and boosts morale; it ensures that the best people do the job; it is part of the training process.

These are all valid reasons for delegating work, although they are often confused with the three underlying principles of dele-gation. This is because we often confuse 'delegation' with 'assignment'. Delegation is part of the process of developing the people of your team, whereas assignment is simply task alloca-tion.

There are three principal reasons for delegation: grooming replacements, getting a better return on your people, and allowing you to focus on high leverage activity.

The need to groom replacements

If you want to be promoted, build depth and talent in your team so that there are a number of people able and willing to take your place whenever the need arises. If you want to spend more time in developing plans to extend existing work or to take advantage of new opportunities, the same thing applies.

When you keep your people shielded from their full potential through some mistaken need for you to be involved in all the important work, you run the real risk of diminishing your colleague's potential and severely limiting your own potential. It is more difficult to promote you if there is no replacement ready to take over from you; in extreme cases your team may collapse into ineffectiveness without you.

Failing to develop replacements is a direct reflection on your ability as a manager and leader. Good people move to positions where they can be challenged. Poor staff stay and, over time, attract more poor staff. Your low opinion of the development potential of your people will be substantiated and you may have to do more and more work to justify your next promotion. This is a downward spiral which will seriously limit your own potential.

Dealing with a failure to groom replacements is often difficult. Established patterns of behaviour are awkward to shift, so it is useful to give this your full conscious attention for a few weeks until new behaviour patterns are learnt. There is no magic formula for making the change, other than to recognise the problem and do something about it. It is always wise, however, to let your colleagues know what you intend and the reason behind it. This way you enlist their support. In making the change, do not be mistaken into thinking that you must be perfect at it first time around. Your first attempts to delegate properly may not work as well as you would like. It is important to know that this is normal and that you will improve with practice.

A better return on your people

Poor performers are the result of low expectations and of leadership without vision or the capacity to challenge people. Top performers look for challenges. When they are not challenged, they find another place to work or else accept second best for themselves.

Your responsibility as team leader is awesome. The growth and development of your colleagues is squarely in your hands. Challenging them with high positive expectations and as much high quality work as you can give them is absolutely essential. This is not achieved by either failing to delegate or by only delegating 'junk work'. Delegation is not 'dumping' or 'trivial pursuit'; it is high value work and an essential part of developing high performance people. If anyone in your team is to be 'underworked', it should be you. This enables you to focus on new products and services, on new approaches to old products, or on new ways of developing your people more effectively.

Focusing on high leverage activity

Effective leaders know that the time they spend on delegation is well spent and an essential element in the performance of their team. They know that short-term commitment to delegating appropriate tasks has a strong, positive long-term effect on performance. A successful delegator is aware that people have their strengths and their weaknesses and that not everything can be done by one person alone. A good delegator knows that there are people in the team who can do a task better than he or she can. The successful delegator relies on that strength and builds on it, and uses delegation to develop weaknesses into strengths, taking great pride in the performance of the team and of the people in it.

THE STRUCTURE OF DELEGATION

The detail necessary to render a delegated task fully effective varies with the complexity and significance of the task and the skill of the person to whom it is delegated. For the simpler tasks, there may be little need to do more than engage in simple conversation, making sure that performance standards and completion deadlines are clear. It is worthwhile remembering, that for the more important tasks, delegation is the art of achieving predefined specific results through the motivation and empowerment of others. Sharing power with other people through delegation is based on an awareness of the following basic steps:

- define the task to be delegated;
- decide to whom it is to be delegated;
- decide when the task is to be completed;
- decide on the way responsibility is to be shared;
- provide the proper authority with which to complete the task;
- insist on a process of accountability and control; and
- identify feedback and reward.

Defining the task

From the start be as precise as you can be about the outcome of the delegation. Be clear about your completion standards, and the form and quality of the outcome expected. Let your colleague know when you think it should be completed and the way the task contributes to the team and to your organisation. Relate the task to the vision of the team and to the business needs of the organisation. With tasks that relate to the agreed development plan for your team member, it is as well to make this clear at the outset of the delegation. Above all be clear about how the task fits into the overall pattern of client relationships in your organisation. One of the misunderstood basic tenets of survival in the long haul for any organisation is how every person and every task relates to client satisfaction and to the competitive advantage this provides.

Prescribing the means by which you expect the outcomes to be achieved, other than in the most exceptional circumstances, seriously limits the creativity and inventiveness of the team member. It also diminishes the development opportunity of the delegation. Delegating the outcome alone leaves your team member free to utilise all their talent and ingenuity in order to reach that outcome. Limiting creativity by prescribing the means reduces the opportunity for learning.

Feedback is most valuable when it is precise and personal and direct. This applies equally to appreciative feedback or corrective feedback. For feedback to be effective you must give it yourself as soon as you discover the activity or performance that prompts it. Feedback should not be delegated.

Deciding to whom to delegate

It is important to know the qualities of the person to whom the task is to be delegated. This is why it is necessary to know what experience and skills your colleagues have, and what degree of independence they are likely to exert. It is important to understand how creative they will be, what level of support they expect, how the task contributes to their development and what training they might need. Once this is understood your communication with them should be clear and without any hidden agendas. Your trust in them should be absolute and your expectations of their performance high and positive. Any training required should be provided in order to properly support them in the task.

The time for completion

Once you have established what the task is and who will undertake it, it is necessary to say when you want the task to be completed. This deadline may be either quite precise or flexible, depending on the circumstances.

For longer and more complex projects you may want to establish additional control or check points:

- milestones at which you want to be informed of progress and beyond which your colleague may not pass until you have had a chance to check on progress;

- specific commitments you may wish to impose as the task progresses.

The degree of control will depend upon the overall importance and complexity of the task. It will also depend on the relative competence of your colleague in the task, and his or her motivation for it.[2] It is very important not to overreact and impose more control than is necessary. In general, the lighter the rein, the more certain the learning.

How responsibility is to be shared

Responsibility for the work of a team, department or organisation always rests with you as leader. It is important, however, to share as much responsibility with your people as possible. Delegation is a process of sharing leadership and responsibility. When this is not done, you diminish the value of the task and delegation becomes task assignment, 'dumping' or 'trivial pursuit'.

There are two key things to do to ensure that delegation is a genuinely shared responsibility. First, publicly praise any outcome that has been done well, attributing it directly to the team member or members who carried it out. Second, publicly accept the responsibility for anything that did not work so well. Do this personally without naming the team member with whom you shared the responsibility however strong a role the team member played in it. After all blaming your team member for an error is a poor way of acknowledging poor performance, and makes it clear that you have no real control in your team arrangements. Note how the Westminister doctrine of ministerial responsibility has developed. Initially it meant that a minister took personal responsibility for anything that went wrong in the department even if he or she had no direct involvement or knowledge of it. In extreme cases the minister would offer to resign. Now it seems that ministers feel quite free to publicly blame their departmental officers.

Providing the proper authority

This is one of the things that separates leaders from managers. Leaders give full authority for a delegated task while managers find it difficult to do so. Your team has no power, no real growth or development, unless you give them full authority for doing the task delegated to them. The growth and development of your team is limited when they have to check for 'approval' at regular intervals, when they have to have your signature on a purchase requisition or an invoice, or otherwise seek your 'authority' to act at a number of stages during the delegated task.

Impose too much control and the development of your team member is stifled. In the majority of cases, giving authority means handing over authority for the task to your colleague, subject to whatever milestone and overall performance standards on which you both agree. In a few cases, it may mean carefully defining the areas in which your colleague can act without reference back to you. In other words: let them get on with the task. Your job is to remove the road blocks to top performance, not to increase them.

In practical terms, this means reaching agreement with your team member on the following issues:

- a budget for the task;
- the level of expenditure responsibility within the budget;
- the personal freedom to make decisions;
- the commitment from other individuals and teams; and
- any other relevant aspect of the task.

Once you have given the authority, do not take it back except in exceptional circumstances. Be aware that when you do, you damage the development you intend to foster and may well end up doing the task yourself.

Always assume that your associates and team members are able to handle about twice the level of responsibility and work-load that you would otherwise give them.

Leaders are remembered because they challenge
their people. Managers are often forgotten because
they let their people get away with second best.

Accountability and control

Accountability and control are possibly the most important parts of the delegation process. However you handle the other aspects of delegation, always make sure the process of accountability is clear. The two principles to be aware of are:

- you share responsibility for a task with your team member, and
- your team member is wholly accountable to you for the results of the delegation.

The process of accountability is where the lessons are learnt and the growth and development occurs. If you expect top quality performance in your team, make sure the agreements and commitments about your outcomes are met.

The four imperatives of accountability are: feedback, training, support and encouragement.

Use the re-submission system outlined in chapter 10, 'Action planning—organising your day', to make absolutely sure that key delivery dates are not missed. A file or reminder note for each major milestone in your re-submission system ensures that the importance you attach to a delegation is not lost in the pressure of the moment. Put a reminder note in your re-submission system a day or so in advance of a critical deadline. Use it to remind yourself to drop by the team member and offer support and inquire about progress.

Through effective use of the re-submission system earn a reputation as 'a leader who never forgets'. This is part of the toughness it takes to be truly effective in drawing your people to enhanced levels of performance.

Involvement in delegation—a critical step

The most effective way to bind your team members to a delegated task is to properly involve them in all the various stages of the delegation process. This is done by asking them for their input on the six stages of the delegation process: definition of outcome, person to whom the task is delegated, time for completion (with milestones), how responsibility is to be shared, the authority necessary, the review or accountability and control necessary and identifying feedback and rewards.

When your team members respond, negotiate agreement on each point by agreeing with as many of their suggestions as possible. Do this even if a suggestion is not quite ideal. Resist the temptation to criticise. It is far better to reach agreement based on their suggestions, *and for you to hold them to those agreements*, than to impose your own structure. Give them the widest possible responsibility for achievement, and thus, for reaching their own potential. Once agreement has been reached in this manner, ask them to prepare a checklist of activities based on your agreement. Use this as the basis for making certain that the reviews are held and that the various performance agreements are met or appropriately renegotiated.

142

THE SIX ATTITUDES THAT INHIBIT DELEGATION

In my seminars on leadership I often ask my group to discuss why it is that they chose not to delegate, or why they do not delegate as much as they really could. The reasons offered are many and varied and most relate to personal 'control' issues or the ego of the delegator. More specifically, the reasons why many people seem reluctant to delegate fully can be defined by six main themes:

- the chosen person does not have the skill and cannot be trained;
- lack of confidence in the person;
- the person's lack of 'understanding';
- the team member needs more training;
- I can do it faster myself; and
- occupational paranoia.

When you think the person chosen or available *does not have the skill and cannot be trained*, it is likely that this is an excuse rather than a reason. In my experience I have found that, provided you are prepared to put the time and energy into your people, there is always something you can do to provide that special environment in which people find the motivation to extend themselves. In one consulting assignment to a large government department I had a chance to demonstrate this very point. A small number of older staff who had been trained under the 'old way' refused to adapt to the new. 'It was good enough in the past, why should I change? In any event, I have only five years to go before I retire . . .', was the common attitude. Their example was demotivating for the younger and more committed staff and frustrating for their managers. There seemed to be no way to deal with them and the more senior managers were quite resigned to their problem.

Based on my belief about individual motivation, I suggested that the department try a different approach. It involved their 'lemons', one at a time, in a series of special teams charged with a closely defined outcome. The result was that each team outperformed the rest of the department within the term of the special exercise. The 'lemon' was indistinguishable from his or her fellow team members. The department manager publicly rewarded the team performance, thereby reinforcing the experience for the entire department, as well as for the special team.

One of the great challenges of leadership is to spend the time

143

and creative energy in challenging people to new levels of achievement and not letting them make do with second best. Quite simply, one way or another, you should have no people in your team to whom you cannot delegate, simply because they have not the skill or cannot be trained.

When you have *no confidence* in a team member it is often because of a past experience when they did not perform to expectation or in some way let you down. Look again at that earlier experience and discover the extent to which you contributed directly to the poor performance. As delegation is an integral part of the training of team members, the trainer bears a key responsibility for the performance.

The solution here is to delegate more rather than less, imposing a tighter control if necessary. It is ultimately counter-productive if an initial failure to perform prevents you from delegating further to any one member of your team.

Maintain your high level of positive expectations of everyone, together with your trust in your people.

Early in my career as a senior manager, I often had the feeling, that my colleague really *did not understand what I wanted to achieve*. Then I learnt that it was far more effective to give a simple, straightforward explanation of the outcome and ask my colleague to repeat the explanation in his or her own words. This reinforced the completeness of the mutual understanding. With more complex tasks, I sought a recapitulation from my colleague at the end of each major element of the total task definition. Whenever there was some discrepancy between what I understood and what my colleague repeated back to me, the ensuing discussion was confined to the area of apparent misunderstanding. I did not waste time with boring and confusing repetition.

In my seminars and my consulting work, I find that most managers relate quite strongly to this experience. It is, after all, the underlying force behind the simple messages of *The One Minute Manager*.[3]

When the person to whom you want to delegate work *needs more training*, the imperatives are simple. Identify the training need, source it, and make sure the training occurs in a timely fashion. Training staff for new tasks is a continuing process carried out by a good leader; remember that often the most effective training is that carried out on the job.

The great trap in delegating is the belief that *you can do it faster and better yourself*. This is not always accurate and is almost always the result of a mistaken focus on the short term rather than the long term. The long-term advantages of keeping your eye on the 'big picture' and developing skills in your colleagues always outweigh the short-term costs of explaining and coaching.

The disease of *occupational paranoia* is an attitude that Ayn Rand[4] once described as the vilest act known to mankind—to hold back another's performance in order to advance your own position. Your role as leader is to challenge each of the members of your team to out-perform you, and to provide the opportunity for them to be promoted out of your team and above you, if appropriate. To do any less is to limit your own performance as leader and to develop mediocrity rather than excellence in your team.

When you rejoice as the leader of a team of champions you reach fulfilment as a leader. When your team is known as the training ground of champions you need have no fear for your future. You are a true achiever.

RISK, MISTAKES AND GROWTH

Contained or well managed, risk is an essential part of the leadership of a team of champions. If you discourage risk, you reduce innovation; without innovation you entrench mediocrity, and championship performance is simply not possible.

There are risks associated with new ventures, with new approaches to old activities, with new and innovative ways to deal with changes to client needs, or to create competitive advantage and respond to the trends in national and international economics. All risk carries the possibility, indeed the near inevitability, of mistakes. Mistakes are the basis of learning in an organisation, and of the growth and development of its people. When mistakes are made as the result of team members risking a new approach or stretching themselves to higher levels of performance, they should be celebrated.

Openness and honesty about mistakes provide the basis of continued development in performance. If your team members are not making any mistakes, you have a team that is not taking risks and not growing. It is quite disastrous if your attitude to mistakes in a learning situation is so severe that mistakes are buried or hidden from you.

Leadership is about ensuring that you have a team environment in which measured or contained risk is a part of the fabric of your team culture and the positive way you deal with it is an integral part of the development of your team.

CONCLUSION

Effective delegation is an essential part of leadership. It is also a vital part of your own development as a leader, as well as being essential to the development of each member of your team.

Delegation is high leverage activity. The extent to which you are able to make choices about spending more time in properly delegating quality work to your team, in developing solution-oriented people, is directly related to your success and achievement as a leader.

KEY MESSAGES FROM CHAPTER 9

- *Your capacity as a leader, to lift you and your team to higher levels of performance, depends on your ability to delegate effectively.*

- *Delegation is about relationships with your colleagues. Through high positive expectations and by stretching your colleagues you can develop solution-oriented people.*

- *Share responsibility in a delegated task; never give away accountability.*

- *Delegation is high leverage activity. It helps you groom replacements and build depth in your team, it provides a better return on your people and gives you time to focus on the key planning and development issues of importance to your team.*

- *A good leader knows how to overcome the major problems in attitude which inhibit successful delegation and has the ability to lift performance in people. The twelve steps to successful delegation are:*

  1 **Set a clear objective** *Do this through discussion concentrating on outcomes rather than on the means by which the task should be achieved. Ask your team members for a short written summary so that you can check on their understanding of the desired outcome.*
  2 **Select the delegate** *Understand what skills training and level of experience you require.*
  3 **Train if necessary** *Make sure you identify any training gaps*

146

in the delegate and provide the necessary training at the appropriate time.

4 **Obtain input from your team member on the process** *Always ask for comments and reaction from your team member. Ask how the task can be undertaken. Support him or her and make suggestions if necessary. Do not dominate. You are the coach.*

5 **Assign the task, indicating deadlines, overall time frame, and milestones** *Ask your team member what the overall expectation should be, and what milestones exist. Use the response as the basis for negotiation, rather than imposing your view.*

6 **Provide guidance as appropriate** *Be open to two-way feedback. Watch for signs of achievement and appreciate the other person's contribution. Use this as an opportunity to 'be available' for guidance if it appears necessary. Do not dominate. Suggest.*

7 **Make up a delegation checklist for each task** *Ask your delegate to complete a checklist for the task. Negotiate around this rather than impose detailed constraints of your own. Allow your delegate to achieve within a general framework of high positive expectations.*

8 **Establish controls** *Make sure you know about progress, so that you can support and guide when necessary.*

9 **Maintain controls** *Once the control steps are established, maintain them. Be open to a reasonable renegotiation. Maintenance of controls is the basis for your feedback on performance. Be tough. Be fair.*

10 **Provide feedback** *Support and appreciate honest effort. Reward achievement. Praise and encourage the risk takers. Respond positively to honest mistakes. Use your observations about performance not directly related to the result to reinforce your high expectations.*

11 **Identify lessons** *Learn and teach from each experience. Be open to feedback from your team member. Discuss what the delegate can learn from the experience. Ask what you did to contribute to any misunderstanding about the performance, and explore what you both learnt about the task and about your relationship in the delegation.*

12 **Evaluate performance overall** *Give a full qualitative and quantitative evaluation of the task. Be careful to use your evaluation to support the overall performance. Look for ways in which specific performance might be improved next time for both of you. Support high expectations and give public praise.*

CHAPTER 10

Action planning— organising your day

A vision without a task is but a dream.
A task without a vision is drudgery.
A vision with a task is the hope of the world.

Church inscription, Surrey, England,
dated 1730

Now, this moment, is where the action is. No amount of vision, goal setting, or planning has any value unless it is reflected in action. Creating a vision and setting goals are the critical first steps towards top performance. Having a vision without a daily action intent, however, is like leaving it all to chance.

If you want to improve your performance radically, drive the process of realising your goals as much from your conscious mind as possible and create a detailed daily action commitment. This reinforces the subconscious power of visioning, increases focus and sense of purpose, and improves performance.

In my seminars, I have observed that many people have a strong aversion to a significant degree of 'organisation'. This resistance is often excused as being in the interests of flexibility. It is interesting to note that the resistance always surfaces at the point where we begin to talk about 'making it all happen'. The difficulty people seem to have with focusing through conscious goal setting clearly pre-exists. Putting it all into practice through 'organising' a day in a reasonably detailed fashion, causes a subconscious reaction to rise to conscious attention. This reaction is stated as a need for flexibility, whereas it is more likely a reflection of an inherent 'fear' of failure (or success).

My response to protests of this kind is that organising my day is the very basis of my capacity to react intelligently to the many opportunities that occur—the basis of my flexibility. When I plan my day, I do so in order to reflect my goals. I react to a new opportunity on the basis of the relative priorities of my plan and of the new opportunity. If the new task is more important to me than the one I have planned, I juggle my schedule to suit the new need. If it is less significant to me, I assign it to another day, or reject it outright. Because I organise my day I know immediately whether the opportunity is of real rather than apparent value to me. I am confident about whether to say 'yes' or 'no' in response to an opportunity. If I were not so clearly focused, I might take up an 'opportunity' that turns out to be of little value. To me this is real flexibility.

The essence of this chapter is providing some simple techniques of organisation which will clarify a strong positive alignment between your goals and what you actually do.

FOCUSING YOUR ENERGIES

This subheading is a reminder that action planning or organising your day is the essential link between focus, vision and goal setting, and the results you want.

Organising your day is begun by setting aside time, on a regular basis, for drawing information from all your projects and translating this into a *specific action to be undertaken at a specific time (day)*. This action derives from many sources: project folders, planning notes, minutes of meetings, directions from within your organisation, and imperatives of one kind or another from your clients.

Each evening, just before I finish for the day, I review the tasks not done and decide when the next action on them should take place. This forms part of my review of the following day's commitments and generally takes ten to fifteen minutes. When I have overlooked some critical preparation for the next day it may take longer. I review my level of commitment and adjust my priorities accordingly. In organising my day I work on the basis of planned 'under-commitment and over-achievement'. Too often I see clients who work in the opposite way to this principle: they over-commit and, inevitably, under-achieve, much to the dissatisfaction of their clients and colleagues.

Having studied a large number of people in a wide variety of business and professional activity, my observation is that, properly motivated, the people who plan their day so as to appear under-committed far out-perform those who are over-committed. The reason for this is simple. When you over-commit, you do not, by definition, meet all your commitments. Whatever your con-

149

scious awareness, there is always an inner or subconscious sense of incompletion and a general feeling of dissatisfaction with your own performance. Often this is reflected in a feeling of unworthiness which affects performance in a cumulative way. There may well be some disgruntled colleagues or clients actively supporting this. Worse, you may even 'enjoy' a reputation for being disorganised and unable to meet your commitments. Your challenge in improving your performance is to ignore this feeling and consciously commit yourself to new and improved behaviour.

Once a week, usually on Thursday evening, I review the tasks and activity planned for the next full week. (Flexibility is the key here. If Thursday is committed in some special way, this activity might occur on a Wednesday, Friday, or at the weekend. Only in very rare circumstances is the review ommitted.) Again I assess commitment levels overall and adjust priorities against my overall goals. In this weekly session, I also review all my major goals and plans, specifically to ensure that activity necessary for maintaining momentum is properly scheduled into my diary and re-submission systems.

Every one or two months I conduct a major 'spring clean' of all files, notes and projects. I look closely at plans and implementation strategies to ensure there is completeness and continued relevance to my goals. All major goals are reviewed in the same manner. Once each six months or so I re-examine my vision and values to ensure that they continue to develop as my own interests, research and experiences indicate.

THREE KEY PRINCIPLES

There are three key principles to organising a day in the most effective way. The first is based on a common attitude towards time. I call this the deficit/surplus principle. The second is our old friend Pareto and its application to action planning on a daily basis. The third is called the clean desk principle.

The deficit/surplus principle

In discussion with my clients and the people who attend my seminars, I have observed that a majority of people operate in what I call 'deficit' in relation to time. They never seem to have enough time to do all the things they want. They spend their time on other people's projects before their own. They allow telephone

150

interruptions and 'drop-ins' to take attention from their true focus. They do their 'priority' work at the end of the day when they are at their least efficient. They take work home or 'run out of time' and 'reschedule' it for tomorrow, over-committing their tomorrows in an exponential way.

In short, they exhibit a 'deficit mentality' about time. They become over-committed and feel bad about not meeting their commitments. Much of this is subconscious, although its conscious form shows up at home, away from the office, where they might experience unaccounted mood swings or general unease. Prolonged deficit mentality about time can lead to anxiety and depression thus creating a more general lowering of performance.

You are too important a person to continue to treat yourself in this way. Change your attitude about your relationship with time by changing your behaviour. Each day, schedule, as a matter of course, the first one-and-a-half to two hours as your own quality time, uninterrupted by telephones and drop-ins except under the most exceptional circumstances. Then you are free to make the remainder of your time available to your clients, colleagues and support staff. This leads your subconscious mind to a surplus view of time.

The reality behind this change is that we have choices about what we do with our time. To be in surplus about time, to feel good about yourself and what you achieve, is to take the decision that you are the most important person in your own world and to act accordingly. This is not meant to support a selfish inward-looking attitude. The point is that if you do not look after yourself and return to surplus in your attitude towards time, you are not truly able to support your team and your organisation in the most appropriate way. Living in deficit will ultimately destroy the value you try to create.

It is equally simple to turn a deficit attitude about money into surplus. Deficit thinking is based on the notion that we give the first portion of our wage or salary to the taxation authorities, the next to banks, finance companies or landlords for mortgages, hire purchase or rent and leasing arrangements. Then we provide for food, bills, clothes and school expenses with the last portion assigned to savings, holidays and 'ourselves'. Changing attitudes about money requires a change in behaviour: give the first 10 per cent of your gross salary, wage or stipend to yourself. This is the basis of the principle of tithing. People who tithe attest to the value of doing so, whether they do so to themselves, their church or an organisation.

A behaviour change in which you give to yourself either time or money, changes your attitude about these 'scarce' resources and you see that you have a choice. Productivity is positively affected by the different attitude. Certainly this is my own experience.[1]

The Pareto principle

The Pareto principle operates in two quite powerful ways in relation to organising your day effectively. First you can choose what time of day to allocate to yourself as quality time and, second you can choose, what you do in that time.

It is important therefore to recognise in which two-hour period you function most effectively and when your creative and productive juices are in full flow. For me it has always been early morning, from seven to nine o'clock. I have found that early morning up to 10 a.m. is quite a common peak performance time. Many people I have spoken to mention a 'second wind' in the early evening and this most closely represents their Pareto time. A few people identify late morning and fewer again immediately after lunch.

It is not always possible in all work environments to preserve this two-hour period, although I have heard of senior executives who do so religiously. The point of scheduling a two-hour period in a routine way is that it is a planned commitment to quality activity. Be aware that, when changing your behaviour, previous subconscious patterns of behaviour will conspire quite creatively to draw you back to old and less productive behaviour. It may require a strong and conscious focus to maintain your Pareto time for the first three or four weeks.

Without this planned commitment you may undertake key productive activity on an ad hoc basis and not necessarily at your most productive time. You may even find you that it is not done at all or that it becomes an urgent or crisis activity.

Whatever time you set aside as your Pareto time, this is the time to write into your diary as the first 'gift' of time. Do this for each day and plan your work carefully so that, as far as practicable, the high leverage work you do is dealt with in this time. Consciously use the time for activity that requires concentrated effort. Having made this commitment, you are still free to make quality choices about new opportunities that come your way. You are much better placed to decide about the best use of your time in the new circumstances.

Once you have made the commitment to Pareto time and carefully planned the activities most appropriate to it, you will find it useful, if not essential, to maintain that time as an interruption-free zone as much as practicable. If you are task-oriented, this concentration on maintaining a two-hour block free of interruptions will provide little or no difficulty. If you tend to be more people-oriented, it will be much more difficult to protect yourself against interruptions.

There are a number of apparently very sensible reasons for allowing interruptions to occur. The one I hear quite often in my seminars is the need to be accessible to clients and staff. Being accessible to clients is, after all, is the essence of good client relationships and being accessible to colleagues and support staff is integral to good management.

In assessing the relative priority of interruptions, it is as well to see 'accessibility' in its correct perspective. One client of mine registered that telephone calls consumed, on average, 60 per cent of total work time for a large group of people dealing with client inquiries. Two major inefficiencies resulted. The first was that staff had little or no time for the follow-up work generated by the telephone calls. Second, the time spent on telephone calls seriously jeopardised attention given to written inquiries and so there was a backlog of many months' work. There was no balance between telephone and written inquiries, and quality was only associated with the 'service' in very rare cases. Much of my advice was concerned with dealing with the telephone callers in a more specialised way, thus leaving the remaining staff exclusively devoted to written work.

Another client was managing an organisation in which there were a number of key directional issues involving a few quite senior colleagues. As he believed strongly in an 'open door' policy in relation to his colleagues, he spent a lot of his time answering their questions and discussing key issues with them—so much so that he had no time to bring those key issues to a conclusion. When I introduced him to the concept of blocking out regular Pareto time, he jumped at the idea. He set aside three hours: one hour was spent on planning his day and dealing with routine matters, and a key two-hour period was set aside immediately afterwards for key planning and development activity. The rest of his time he spent either in his office, with the door open,

153

working on less significant issues or discussing issues with his senior colleagues and key staff members.

The change required full communication and understanding with a number of key people. He let the people most affected by his new pattern of work know what the changes were, why they were made, the benefits for them, and what changes they had to make to support him. He reached an understanding with his close colleagues about issues on which he could be interrupted. His personal assistant also played a key part in the change. Between them, for example, they developed procedures for making sure he followed up promptly with people who called when he was unavailable. The result was a significant improvement in performance and an increase in his own sense of achievement.

Another reason I hear in my seminars for not putting aside time each day that is free of interruptions is that it is just not possible to do so. I encourage people with this view to think that they cannot afford *not* to put aside at least an hour each day. Most of them absent themselves from their work place for meetings with clients or suppliers, for holidays, or even for personal shopping, and this is perfectly well justified. It then becomes a matter of choice and routine.

If you genuinely cannot find two hours free of interruptions in your own work place, find time away from it for your Pareto activity. Work at home if you are likely to be uninterrupted there, or use an empty office or some other refuge at work that serves the particular purpose. When you do this, ensure that your personal assistant knows where you are and for what particular purposes you can be interrupted.

The clean desk principle

In organising your day it is important to operate in a way that allows you *to start and end the day with a clean desk.* During the day, only those papers that relate to the work you have committed to do that day are on your desk: no in-tray, no pending tray, no carry-over files or papers. My own preference is to have my desk clear of papers except for those on which I intend to work that day, and to use a completely clear conference table to work on, concentrating on *one issue at a time.*

The first reason why a clean desk is important, is the considerable, subconscious, negative impact of a cluttered desk—the large number of incompletions represented by files and papers you can have no chance of addressing that day. You can judge this negative impact best by the way you feel when you return to your office after an absence of a week or so. There is a feeling of anxiety, or even momentary depression, as the impact of the incomplete work hits you.

Another good reason for keeping a desk clear relates to the distraction a cluttered desk provides as you conduct your normal business. If a distraction has nothing to do with what you have *planned* to do that day, you can easily allow yourself to stray widely from what is important. A positive performance-oriented attitude is ensured when your desk has on it only those things that are important during the day, and when you have a clear desk each morning and evening.

This positive attitude reinforces values about the need for daily planning. A complete planning activity (vision, values, goals, objectives and the daily planning process) is directed towards focusing *action* on the activity of a particular day. To have anything else on my desk at any one time other than those things which relate to my plan for the day disrupts my concentration and my focus on what is important.

In talking to people in my seminars, I have discovered why many people treat their desktops as open filing cabinets. They feel that having all possible action files on their desks gives them a reassurance that nothing will be overlooked. They seem to sense that, when files and other action reminders are tucked away in filing cabinets, cupboards or drawers, they are in some sense 'out of control'. They are vaguely aware of something that has to be done and cannot quite remember what it was.

I have noticed, however, that the action item which is certain not to be overlooked is the one on the top. If you have four piles of paper on your desk, four actions attract your attention. Unless you spend a regular session on culling all files for priority order and action, that sense of incompleteness will remain. For the most part, having piles of paper irrelevant to your daily plan on your desk almost guarantees you will overlook something.

Another view that seeks to justify holding a large array of papers and action reminders on a desk, lies in the argument: 'I need this at arm's reach in case I have a telephone call about it.' This is often fallacious. When large numbers of files are 'in reach' in this way, it often takes longer to find a particular file than if it were correctly filed in a nearby filing cabinet. It is far better to plan your relationships with clients, suppliers and advisers so that you can anticipate when a call is likely to be made. You are then more likely to have the file on your desk close to the expected time it is needed.

The need therefore is for a system of operating which meets both needs: a clean desk and a sense of security about the way files and action items are stored so that you cannot fail to take action on the right day in relation to that task. By this, I mean having the papers on your desk on the prescribed day in order to take appropriate action. Whether you take that action depends on the circumstances of the day and how they relate to your priorities. This can be done by creating a personal re-submission system.

A PERSONAL RE-SUBMISSION SYSTEM

For me, this is an essential complement to normal work-planning procedures. In larger organisations you may find an elaborate general re-submission system based on your organisation's records management procedures. You should plan to use this to the full, complementing it by developing a simple personal system to further improve your productivity.

A number of alternatives can be used as a personal re-submission system. The one I have found to be the simplest to install and to use is based on a single drawer of a standard filing cabinet. If one is not available, a shelf deep enough to take a foolscap folder with a vertical or side tab can be easily adapted. When I use a drawer, it is set up as a simple hanging file system with 43 files. Twelve files are labelled 'January' through to 'December' and these act as repositories for longer term re-submissions. A further 31 hanging files, labelled '1' to '31', are used to represent the days of the current month. These files contain items of specific action commitment that have been assigned to a specific day.

The system works as a readily accessible reminder system. When you arrive for work on 10 May, for example, you open the drawer and the first hanging file you see is marked '10', representing 10 May. In it are all the papers you have previously assigned to 10 May. This will have been occasioned by some previous review of your action activity. You may have consigned the particular action to that file one or two days previously, or you may have consigned it there a number of months earlier. The point is that these were conscious decisions derived from reviews of your vision, goals and plans. Once you empty the folder '10',

A personal re-submission system

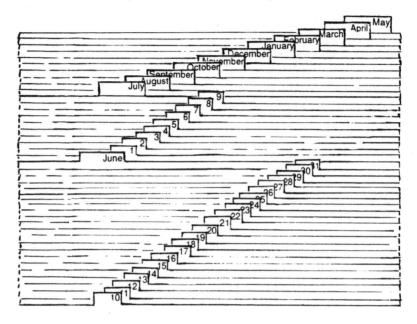

it is placed back into the drawer behind the folder marked '9' where it now represents 10 June.

For a particularly bulky file, replicate the key information about it—topic, context, key players and phone numbers, etc.—on a piece of board paper and use that in your filing drawer re-submission unit. The bulky file is then stored in another filing cabinet or cupboard and the reference location is noted on the paper in your own re-submission system.

The re-submission system has value far beyond action reminders about files and projects. Use it to follow-up on delegations, requests for information, and on clients and suppliers. Use it also for reminders on cyclical actions such as regular monthly commitments, annual bonus and salary reviews, the initiation of budgetary reviews and other business planning processes. Use it also for a range of personal matters: reminders about birthdays, social events, theatre engagements and periodical payments such as rent, rates and subscriptions. Its use is only limited by your imagination and your circumstances.

I have used this system in a number of business contexts and in each it has been worth two to three hours a day in improved productivity. There is no more unnecessary reliance on memory, or worry or anxiety about completion or meeting commitments made. There is an increased focus on what is important *right now*.

When you put action items away into the system, particularly if the issue is complex and there is more than a little time until the next action point, you will find it useful to write a little note to yourself on a self-adhesive note and attach this to the file. This puts you in the picture the minute you pick the file out of the re-submission system.

The general or monthly files, those marked 'January' through to 'December', are sorted towards the end of the previous month as part of your regular monthly forward planning activity.

The system takes a little while to set up, perhaps half a day or so. You will find this is best done one Saturday or Sunday morning, away from the normal activity of a busy work environment. Initially it takes more than a little commitment to make it work. Old patterns tend to return readily and some positive reinforcement and dedication is necessary at first, but in a very short period of time you will find it works well and takes only a few moments each day to keep it operating. The re-submission system works at top efficiency if it is implemented on a no-exception basis. A number of times during my consulting work it has become clear to me that partial use of the system is quite distracting. When everything is in the system as a matter of practice, there is a greater certainty about the way it works.

A personal re-submission system such as this is an essential element in keeping your desk clear of all papers other than those with which you want to deal on a particular day. Using the system creates a certainty in your mind that tasks that need to be addressed at some future specific date will be brought to your attention at the appropriate moment. This frees your mind, your energy and your enthusiasm for the specific tasks at hand. It creates, in turn, greater productivity for you and your organisation.

MAKING YOUR DAY WORK FOR YOU

Creating a structure for your day operates as a framework for positive and flexible response to the demands of an increasingly complex work environment. The aim is to have your day work for you rather than the reverse.

Preparation

The day begins last thing the night before when you glance at your diary to review what you plan for the following day. This reminds you of any preparation you have to do before the day begins; what papers you have to take home to prepare for that early morning meeting; what information is necessary for a presentation you are giving; what special commitments you have that may necessitate a change from your normal routine; what special task you have scheduled that might require you to give advanced thought to it.

If you are better tuned to this review in the morning, make sure you arrive early enough to do it before the formal part of the day begins. Even so always glance at your diary the night before to make sure that there are no surprises. It is nice to learn the night before that your first appointment the next day is 40 kilometres away from the office, rather than learn three minutes before the appointment that it is not in your work area.

When you arrive the next day you are fully prepared for the day ahead. You arrive at a clean desk knowing your principal tasks for the day and the general sequence in which you will work. Look again at your diary as you arrive to fully apprise yourself of the day ahead.

Getting started

Your first task is to collect the contents of the relevant file from your re-submission drawer and place these papers with the contents of your 'in-tray'. It makes good sense to have this sorting and decision-making process out of the way as expeditiously as possible. If you are a late starter or likely to be away from your work space or office first thing in the morning, you may find it useful to undertake this review last thing the night before.

This early morning decision making is a time when the tone of the day is set. Being decisive at this point sets up the rest of the day for you—within the context of your committed block times. It removes any tendency to shuffle pieces of paper from one heap on your desk to another, particularly if they represent tasks about which you intend to do nothing. The HEPOPOO principle is a useful guide: **H**andle **E**ach **P**iece **O**f **P**aper **O**nly **O**nce—at each action point.

There are a number of alternatives when dealing with the combination of paper from your re-submission file and your in-tray. Each will decide what the priorities for the day will be. Remember, just because you previously committed yourself to handling an issue on a particular day does not mean it is still appropriate to do so. A review of priorities sets up the day properly.

One decision-making structure of great simplicity is to divide your papers or action possibilities into these categories:

- Must do today.
- Must do on another day.
- Must read.
- Junk.

The junk file is put straight into the waste bin. The reading file is put aside to a special time each week that you have committed to essential reading. The 'must do another day' file is put into your re-submission drawer. The 'must do today' file is put into priority order, relating the tasks to your other 'block' commitments for the day.

Another slightly more sophisticated system is to categorise your tasks in the following way:

1 *Do it now* This includes the sorting of papers as a whole. Other more specific actions include noting comments, instructions, requests, etc., on the original of the received document and forwarding it to the action person; copying an important piece of information for your records; calling for a back-up file; or arranging a quick meeting with a colleague. This is all part of the good practice of HEPOPOO. Annotating original correspondence saves a lot of time. Similarly, using handwritten responses on an incoming fax as the basis of a return fax is increasingly used in all manner of business contexts, both internal and external. This practice carries with it considerable productivity gains, although it is resisted in some organisations on the grounds of its informality.

2 *Do it later today* These involve placing the relevant paper in its file in priority or time order on your desk top. This constitutes part of your 'agenda' for the day and its proper place is on your desk.

3 *Call for information/reports by . . . and deal with it then* This category involves writing a note on the original with your request (including the date due), forwarding the original to the person providing the information, and putting a copy in your re-submission file to ensure follow-up.

4 *Do it on . . . when I am free to give it my fuller attention* Put the papers into your re-submission file at the appropriate date, preferably with a note as to what action you intend to take at that point. This should not be confused with procrastination. Often a task can legitimately be dealt with more effectively at a later date. This might be because you will have more information then or because your priorities genuinely indicate the necessity to work on something more important now. Sometimes I find it useful to put papers like this into my re-submission file a day or so before the action day. This is to give me a chance to review the file and decide what preparation might be necessary so that I may address it more expeditiously on the allotted day.

5 *Delegate to . . . to handle this matter by . . .* . For simple delegated tasks, write a note on the original and send it to the person who will be responsible for the task. Place a copy in your re-submission file if you want to follow up on it. For more complex matters the delegation structures described in chapter 9 on 'Developing Your Team through delegation' are appropriate.

6 *Not necessary to be done and not useful as information for me or my team* Throw them away. If you have strong bowerbird tendencies, put a marginally relevant piece of information into your re-submission drawer two or three months ahead. When it re-emerges you will wonder what possessed you to keep it.

Dealing promptly with these papers at the start of the day takes the majority of them off your desk and to the appropriate action point. Whether this point is the waste bin, your assistant, colleague or your re-submission system, the important point is that it frees your mind to focus on what is important.

Your desk is clear and all tasks assigned to other days will come back to your attention on the appropriate day. Follow-up procedures have been taken care of effectively. Over the years I have observed that follow-up is one area in which many managers, including senior executives, 'drop the ball'. If you fail to follow up activity that is important to you, you may be perceived as regarding it as unimportant. Just saying it is important at the outset diminishes in value over time and is far less effective than giving a task a specific time for follow-up and completion.

Attention given early in the day to the re-submission system rarely takes more than a few minutes. Its value is that it allows you to concentrate fully on the tasks you have planned with your

161

priorities properly in mind. This leaves you with a strong feeling of being in control, leading to increasing energy and enthusiasm.

OTHER ASPECTS OF ORGANISING YOUR DAY

Principal among the opportunities for productivity improvement in daily planning are preparation for major activity, the use of telephones, dealing with incoming mail and dictation.

Planning for major activity

Your Pareto time has already been set aside in your diary. Your weekly and daily preparation will have ensured that the most important activity has been scheduled to be done in that time. Most importantly, you will have made arrangements to ensure that your Pareto time is uninterrupted.

There are other tasks you may wish to group together and perform in a particular block of time. These might include telephone calls, dictation and the walking around time so necessary in effective leadership. 'Blocked' times will already have been set aside for meetings and interviews.

A short period of time set aside for preparation is useful before each meeting and interview. Similarly, planning for a short time after a meeting to properly record any necessary action as a result of the meeting is valuable. Carefully planning travel time in relation to meetings and interviews away from the office is also useful. Take some work with you so that if you arrive early or your meeting is delayed, you make good use of your waiting time. This is part of under-committing and over-achieving, and of high performance.

Telephones

Telephone calls are a messy business at the best of times and can, if uncontrolled, run away with your day. One way to bring this into focus is to undertake a regular analysis of the number of calls you make and the length of time you spend on them as a proportion of your overall work.

Making as many outgoing calls as you can at the beginning of the day places you in a good position to meet your plan for the rest of the day. Information is available to you. Meetings have been organised. You have no need to remember to make outgoing

162

calls for the rest of the day. When you fail to make contact, you at least know what you have to do to work around it. To find the other person away from the office when the call is left to the last minute can be embarrassing.

What works well for me is to make a few calls immediately after I have sorted through my paper work. After lunch I make a few more calls and repeat the most important calls I made that morning if they have not been returned. If I find that the other person is away from the office I make an immediate note in my re-submission drawer or diary to call again on the next day he or she is available. I always leave a message that I have phoned, making it clear whether I would like a return call or will call again.

There are a number of other significant ways in which you can improve your productive use of the telephone:

- Only make those calls that are absolutely necessary.
- Decide what you want from your phone call before you make it. Write down your objectives prior to the call, particularly if there is more than one.
- Don't gossip. Most people you will call are busy and will appreciate the courtesy you show them when you get straight to the point, address the issue, and sign off. If you want to gossip, say so, and be responsive to the signs you receive from the other person. Be firm and kind about reminding the other person that you are busy, would love to chat further, and will do so at a more convenient moment. A good way to set up the 'no gossip' routine is to announce your purpose and your intention to be businesslike about your call right from the start.
- Screen your incoming calls by having a good understanding with your colleagues or by using a good answering device. You will need to communicate clearly to colleagues a priority list of callers who can interrupt a particular task or who can be redirected to an office you are visiting. In this latter case it is as well to specify from whom you will take calls from and for what purpose. A well-briefed associate can provide much of the information that is sought by the caller without bothering you. This will depend on a close and open working relationship between you and your associate.
- Avoid 'telephone tag'. Telephone tag is that delightful time-wasting trap that it is so easy to fall into, particularly in those less thoughtful moments you experience when you are very busy. 'Tell Jones I called and please ask him to call back', is

followed by a return message: 'Please let Wildblood know that Jones returned his call'. 'Wildblood here. Let Jones know I tried again. Please ask him to call me' . . . and so on. I am not sure what the *Guinness Book of Records* will tell us, although I know of one telephone tag that went on for several weeks without any more information than the names of the two players being transmitted. You only avoid telephone tag by treating the person who answers the phone, or decodes the answering device, as an intelligent human being fully capable of taking and transmitting useful messages. For example, 'Please let Jones know that Wildblood called and that I phoned to inquire about the report on the mailing statistics due next Tuesday. I would like to know whether this is still possible. If you can find out for me and give me a call back that would avoid bothering Jones with another phone call. I'd really appreciate your help as I depend on the information. I'll be in my office until 6.30 this evening. Tomorrow I'll be interstate and then back in the office on Friday. Do you think you will be able to get back to me by then?' In circumstances where the message is more than usually complex or you have a feeling that the message is not fully understood, this might well be followed by: 'This is important for me and I'm never sure how well I communicate under pressure. Perhaps you would be kind enough to repeat to me what you think I have said' . . . or words to a similar effect that work for you. Always leave your full name, company name and telephone number.

- Take notes as you call, particularly for the more involved calls and for those calls when it is important to get it right. Do not hesitate to repeat information you have received from the other person and ask them for confirmation of your understanding of it. 'Let me check that to make sure I have understood you . . .'
- Know when to end your call. This is all part of planning; if you have set a target for your call and its business framework, you will find it easier to terminate the call once you have completed your business.

Telephones are an important part of business life. You owe it to yourself, and to those whom you contact by telephone, to use the telephone in a business-like way. High performance people always plan and control their use of the telephone well.

164

Dealing with incoming mail

The place to rest your in-tray is as far from your work space as possible and preferably outside your office area. I organise my day so that only those things I am dealing with are on my desk. Other papers on it have a strong potential to distract me. The in-tray, because of its volume and potential content, is the worst possible distraction.

When you are concentrating on a task of importance and a letter, file or report hits your desk, there is a temptation to let your eye drift to it. A key word or signature takes your eye. Before you are aware of it, you give that piece of paper all your attention at the expense of something you have previously decided is important to you. This does not mean that the new item is not more important. It may be. The overwhelming likelihood, however, is that it is not and being distracted by it can often seriously affect productivity.

I prefer to have my daily in-tray of internal and external mail left until the following morning when I deal with it first thing on arrival. Having good communication and understanding between you and your personal assistant, and allowing your assistant to receive all correspondence, provides an increased capacity for substantial productivity gains. Your assistant will open your mail as it arrives, interrupt you only in accordance with a set of priorities you have established, arrange file and previous paper attachments, and have it all ready for your evening and early morning attention. If you and your assistant have really worked at communication and understanding, draft answers to letters of a more or less routine nature will arrive attached to your mail, and suggestions for action will be made. You will find additional reports, information or comments from associates affected by the particular communication attached to correspondence without your active intervention.

Addressing your in-tray in one short session places you in a position to deal with it much more effectively and to relate it properly to your organisation for the day.

Dictation

Dictation is an office practice of diminishing significance in many offices. In some work environments it has become a lost art and productivity has become seriously affected. On the other hand, technology has clearly provided productivity gains in other ways and this is sometimes sufficient to outweigh losses through the absence of good dictating practice. In the public services, 'multi-skilling' has resulted in a 'de-skilling' in dictating skills and there has been a consequent loss of productivity. In my consulting work generally I have seen too many occasions where dictation was not used where it might have been more appropriate to use it, or where some of the basics of good dictation were ignored.

Audio dictation is the most efficient. It enables you to dictate independent of your personal assistant or any central secretarial service. You can plan dictation into your day much more efficiently. Your dictation can be uninterrupted and your assistant remains free to concentrate on his or her tasks. Audio dictation can, moreover, be undertaken out of hours when it may be unreasonable for your assistant to be present. Unfortunately, dictation skills in most people are so deficient that one-to-one personal dictation is a significant waste of time for the secretary or personal assistant taking the dictation.

The basic skills of good audio dictation include the following principles:

- Be clear about the purpose of your dictation. Set goals by quickly outlining in advance the sense of the material you wish to dictate. Know the purpose of each piece of dictation. Indicate clearly what information, files or other background materials you need in order to address the matter properly.
- Give clear instructions about the dictation at the beginning of the dictation: anticipated length, format, addressee, number of copies, draft or final copy.
- Speak clearly, without haste, directly into the machine.
- Minimise interruptions during dictation.
- Clearly indicate sentence, paragraph and document endings.
- Dictate only one document on each tape except under the most exceptional circumstances.

If you spend a lot of time out of the office, a portable dictating machine or notepad computer is almost a necessity. Use either tool for drafting notes and reflections in response to client contact. Capture ideas generated by observations elsewhere, or draft substantive reports.

FEEDBACK AND RECOGNITION

Concluding your day appropriately is as important as getting off to a good start. First, it is the basis of the next day's plan. Probably more important is the process of 'parking' the issues and concerns of the day in order to leave you free to enjoy the other things you value in your life: family and social, sporting and recreational activities.

Prior to giving some thought to the next day's planning, it is useful to review the work you have completed that day. Look particularly for the good quality work you achieved, whether or not it was recognised by anyone other than yourself. Give yourself a notional pat on the back for all the excellent work you did. If something went particularly well, set aside time on the way home or first thing next day to buy yourself something special. This is important, essentially because it takes your focus from the *occasional* thing that went badly, something you might otherwise maintain focus on well after you leave your work place. Maintaining a negative focus colours your thinking and this can seriously affect subsequent performance and sense of wellbeing. Full personal recognition of your positive achievements puts a more realistic perspective on your work for the day. It releases positive energy which increases productivity and spills over to favourably affect family and social activity.

In reviewing the day, pause a moment only to reflect on those issues you might have handled better. Ask yourself: What was it that tipped the balance away from a better result? How can I act next time to minimise error or to improve performance? What can I learn about the task, about myself, from my experience? This process takes a minute or two. The rewards for doing so are cumulative and they last for days.

CONCLUSION

The message of this chapter is not structure. It is the use of structure *at those moments when results are of importance to you.* When your sense of priority indicates a need for focus at a particular time, the use of the various suggested techniques provides a basic framework of organisation that works. This framework has worked for me for a number of years and I always adjust it to suit my circumstances. The significance of the framework is its continual focus on results of value, on what I see at any point as important to me.

Planning and structure provide an environment so much more free from time pressures than was ever the case when I lived a

167

'more flexible' and less ordered life. The opportunities I have open up for me like a cornucopia compared to the 'invisible clutter' I tried to make sense of in the past. I seem to have an increased ability to react positively and creatively to the opportunities and challenges that come my way.

My experience suggests, as does that of many of the top performers I know, that structure and planning used appropriately provide a platform from which peak performance can be achieved.

KEY MESSAGES FROM CHAPTER 10

- *Set aside time each week, either Thursday or Friday evening, to plan the coming week. Make sure that you first allocate time to yourself to do those things that are important to you in your work commitments.*

- *Set aside a 10–15 minute period at the end of each day to review what you have achieved, to properly acknowledge it, and to plan for the subsequent day.*

- *Plan for a one to two-hour block of time each day for key planning, organising or other high leverage activities.*

- *Keep yourself from being distracted unnecessarily from what you have planned for the day. Close your door, sit facing away from the door, and keep your in-tray outside your office or work space.*

- *Work towards having only those papers on your desk that relate to your planned commitments for the day. Set up a personal re-submission system to ensure that tasks assigned to a particular day are addressed on that day. Check that your desk/work space is clean and tidy as you leave each day.*

- *For each major activity, set aside time to properly plan its execution. For activities of great significance to you, set aside quiet time immediately beforehand to fully prepare.*

- *Set aside a half hour or so close to the start of each day and again after lunch for outgoing phone calls. Keep track of them and make follow-up calls where appropriate.*

- *At the end of each day spend one or two minutes reviewing possible areas of improvement and acknowledging all those activities that worked to your satisfaction.*

CHAPTER 11
Using your diary

In the previous chapter we saw how important it was to draw from all your ideas, projects and areas of activity and focus on them as a commitment to daily action. Your diary is, among other things, your vehicle for this focus. It is your intent for the day, your commitment to undertake action.

Your diary is a powerful tool for gathering into one place action commitments for daily activity; maintaining momentum on key areas; and creating a positive attitude towards performance.

In this chapter we deal with how to use a diary to maximum effect, the choice of diary, and the relationship between your diary and 'to do' list, and the nature of commitment and the way it underpins successful action focus.

THE MAIN PURPOSES OF A DIARY

There are two principal purposes of a diary. The first is as your daily plan of action and the second is as a record of what actually occurred.

Your diary as a complete daily plan

Your diary page should have two elements. The first is an outline of what is planned *by time of day*. The second is a list of what *particular detailed activity* you plan, whether or not it has a distinct time assigned to it.

169

Diary entries are often made many days in advance of the actual commitment. When circumstances and priorities change, adjustments to the diary are necessary. This is why *using a pencil for all diary entries* makes good sense. Erasing a pencil entry and re-writing the new entry is far tidier and more readable. Ink entries scratched out and over-written tend to look messy and detract significantly from the graphic picture the diary page is meant to provide.

Once you have completed your diary plan for a day, it becomes the measure against which you judge interruptions, or any opportunities that come your way. When an interruption occurs, or when a new opportunity presents itself, you can decide its importance relative to the commitments in your diary. In this way, for example, an unplanned new activity may be judged important enough for you to divert from your plan. You may decide to give it some preliminary time at the point of interruption and return to it another time when you can devote your full attention to it, or you may decide it is sufficiently important to devote a major chunk of time to it immediately.

Dealing with unplanned work by a reasonable assessment of relative priorities tells you what you have to do with your current commitment. It gives you a lot more freedom and flexibility.

Key activities by time-line

The section of your diary page that outlines your major commitments by time of day may include any of the following:

- preliminary planning or organising time;
- your Pareto time and any specific activity planned for it;
- time set aside for meetings, interviews and visits, both regular and ad hoc;
- luncheon arrangements;
- specific block times for telephone calls;
- time for walking around in client liaison and production areas, coaching, supporting, listening for ideas and issues you can turn to your advantage; and
- a specific telephone call or personal matter you have to attend to at a particular time.

This list is not exhaustive; your own circumstances and priorities will dictate what you put in the time-line section.

In making your diary entry it is useful to decide, with reasonable accuracy, how much time you want to spend on each major item. My observation is that, when executives and professional people do this, they become about 15–25 per cent more productive. This is yet another example of the powerful nature of goal setting in improving performance.

Another tip is to avoid underestimating the time you expect to spend on any one commitment. My experience in speaking with executives who have attended my seminars is that there is a strong tendency to do so, particularly in relation to meetings. This causes a cumulative overrun of time, a sense of overcommitment and, hence, lack of accomplishment, of being out of control. If you err on the side of caution about what is reasonable to accomplish, *and make certain that you do what you commit to do*, you focus subconsciously on accomplishment. The panic of overcommitment is replaced by a real sense of achievement.

In any event the preliminary planning you do in deciding your goals and in organising the day will give you a firm framework on which to exercise your choices. For example, indicate a full block of time for a particular activity in the time-line section of your dairy page.

Only indicating a start time is a trap. When you review a diary page, it is easy to lose perspective of the entire anticipated commitment in time. This can lead you to make an additional commitment which, on closer reflection, might clash with the commitment you have. This is why I like to shade my time commitments in pencil and include preparation and follow-up time in the total time commitment. Preparation speaks for itself. If the task is important to you, you will want to do the very best you can and this always requires some preliminary work, even if it is just a short period in which to focus once again on the key objectives of the activity to follow. Sometimes there will be a need for more extensive preparation. The time taken to record any follow-up action is equally important. Leaving it to the end of the day increases the potential for overlooking some key element of activity or losing the subtlety of a key issue not properly recorded at the time.

Planning for preparation and follow-up in this way also provides a buffer for any return phone calls and for those small and important actions that seem to be constantly necessary in most work environments.

Other specific action items

Generally, the more important of your tasks and activities are

entered in the time-line section of your diary. The other major
section of your diary page includes all those actions from your
projects that you have committed to take on the particular day,
other than the major activities you have identified by time-line.
This is your daily 'to do' list. It is a list of all those specific tasks
you intend to accomplish on the day:

- items taken from the day's folder from your re-submission
  drawer;
- telephone calls you intend to make that day;
- follow-up actions: work delegated, information or reports outstanding;
- specific tasks you may wish to accomplish: reports to write,
  letters to finalise, budget information to gather or sales pro-
  jections to work out;
- any personal activity you intend to 'squeeze' into your schedule for the day.

The closer you are to a particular daily plan, the more detailed
it becomes. After you undertake your review last thing at night,
your diary page will represent a full plan for the following day.
All major time commitments will have been entered, as will all
other specific actions deriving from the papers and files you have
consigned to your re-submission folder. Your diary page is then
the focus of your action for the day; everything that is important
is there.

Your diary as a record and review mechanism

Working life is so full of challenges and uncertainties that it is
highly unlikely that the day you completed looks exactly like the
day you planned. Quite legitimately, and within your well articulated goals, things that you had not foreseen presented themselves. Opportunities arose which required scheduled events and
activities to be re-negotiated and entered anew on another day's
plan. A report had to be written under new conditions or time
constraints. An emergency meeting or interview became necessary. Activities you genuinely did not have time for rolled over
to another day. However, take care not to automatically roll
everything undone over to the next day. Each item has its own
most appropriate 'next time' and deciding this time should be a
considered judgement. Automatically dumping incomplete work
from one day to the next quickly leads to chronic overcommitment.

This means that your plan for the day does not represent what you have actually achieved. For your own record purposes, and in order to gain a full sense of achievement, it is important to complete the record. Adjust the time-line section of the diary as well as annotate your daily activity schedule. Erase the time-line entries that did not occur and enter those that did. Translate any activity from your activity schedule that developed into a major task into your time-line record. This is particularly useful if there are large sections of your time-line section without entries. Filling out the time-line framework at the end of the day gives your day substance when you review it. Without it the time-line entry might well look as if little were achieved.

Run through the record version of your diary page time-line section and acknowledge completion of each entry there with a tick (✓). Follow this up with a review of your activity schedule and mark the activities appropriately.

Finally, as an integral part of the planning process for your next day, ensure that you give yourself full recognition for your positive achievements.

CHOOSING A DIARY

How well you use a diary depends on your choice of diary. Many of the diaries available are totally inadequate. This is often because they do not provide enough space to adequately represent a daily plan in useful detail. The poor design of the diary page also contributes to their ineffectiveness.

Your choice is very much dependent on your personal circumstances. A number of my clients find a 'week-at-a-glance' diary essential; many prefer, as I do, a 'page a day' format. There are a number of valuable diaries/planners in that they support goal setting, planning and project work along the lines of the principles set out in this book. They are loose-leaf systems that ensure that regularly used information (addresses, project notes, etc.) move with you from year to year without elaborate end-of-year transfers. There are many such systems available and no one is universally applicable to all work styles. My suggestion is that you assess the requirements you have for page design and then look for an appropriate diary. While doing this, try drawing up a page design of your own in which the distinction between the time-line and the activity list is clear. A sample page is set out on page 174.

Suggested layout for an activity diary page

CALENDAR

Date..

			✓			✓
Ⓛ	A B C		✗	A B C	*Contact:*	✗
	A B C					
8:	A B C					
9:	A B C					
10:	A B C					
11:	A B C			A B C	*Activity:*	
12:	A B C					
1:	A B C					
2:	A B C					
3:	A B C					
4:	A B C					
5:	A B C				*Notes:*	
6:	A B C					
7:	A B C					

USING 'TO DO' LISTS

The only 'to do' list I find of any real value is the daily activity schedule described above. Other than this, I find them a mixed blessing and have certainly seen them become counter-productive. Dumping all your incomplete work onto one list means that there are always many items on it that are not done at the end of the day. Most of them are things you really had no intention of addressing.

They sit there, 'reminding' your subconscious that you have not completed the tasks on your list.

I worked with one client who spoke to me of a constant feeling of frustration with his work. He worked long hours and felt he was efficient at what he did. Yet he always left work with a sense that he had performed poorly. It took me a moment to sense what was wrong. My client had a large whiteboard on his wall on which was listed all his major projects. Each was so complex and long-term that he rarely had an opportunity to cross one off. Rather he found himself adding things to the list. At my suggestion, he transferred all his major projects from the whiteboard to a weekly review file. From this he planned his *daily* 'to do' list which was written on his whiteboard. At the end of each day he erased the specific action items completed. The weekly review of his general project or 'to do' list, which was out of sight, ensured that no specific action of importance was overlooked. My client reported an immediate turn around. His sense of poor performance was replaced by one of real accomplishment. His energy level improved considerably.

Note how the use of a re-submission system would have complemented this process by ensuring that the comprehensive 'to-do' list was not overlooked. My own preference is for using the re-submission system *to remind me of my projects*. In this case I was moving my client from a system that did not work for him to one that was more likely to work for him.

If you do have a 'to do' list that goes beyond a reasonable commitment for a single day, use it as a weekly, or monthly, guide from which you plan your daily commitment list.

A NOTE ABOUT COMMITMENT

Diary systems are the key to action focus. The notion of commitment is integral to successful action and this is why I pause here to consider commitment in more detail.

I use the word 'commitment' frequently. This is because I believe that the notion of commitment is critical to top performance in all aspects of working and personal life. Commitment is one of the keys to improving personal performance. It is important to quality of product or service and to good relationships at any level.

Commitment is about a relationship with yourself. It is also about relationships with other people, and with the team or organisation with which you work. It is a personal, social and family concern as much as it is a business concern.

If you choose not to meet your commitments to yourself and to other people on a regular basis, you develop a conscious or subconscious sense of unworthiness: 'I am a person who does not meet my commitments. I cannot be trusted. I am unworthy' are all expressions of a subconscious message driven home by many such experiences. It is not the kind of internal message that supports high achievement.

Meeting commitments is therefore important. The idea of making a commitment is, however, 'heavy duty' for many people. Indeed, I have known many people, senior executives among them, who spend their lives avoiding commitment. Often the cost of doing this is high. Their personal relationships are poor and achievement against potential is second rate.

One of my notions about commitment is that it means a promise to do something, to take a certain action. It is also a promise to yourself or to others or both; a promise upon which you, and others, depend.

It is important that the notion of commitment is not seen as a framework for inflexibility, that you retain a power of choice in everything you do. When a commitment is genuinely made and something occurs to make it difficult or impossible to meet, a discussion can always be initiated about renegotiating the commitment and its timing. In other words commitments *are* negotiable and, properly undertaken in advance of a deadline, rarely cause any long-term damage to a personal or business relationship. In working with commitment in this way it is vital to address the following questions:

- What flexibility do I have?
- What tolerances are there in my commitment?

176

- What cost, or likely cost, is there to me and to my colleague or client, if the commitment is not met?

The issue is always more readily resolved if the renegotiation occurs before the deadline of the commitment. This indicates respect for yourself, your colleague or your client. It allows greater opportunity for renegotiation and is more likely to leave the relationship intact.

On the other hand, 'renegotiating' a commitment after the event indicates a degree of contempt for the person to whom the commitment is made, and puts you in an adverse position. My experience is that most people, out of some mistaken belief in their ability to achieve miracles, leave the renegotiation to after the event or ignore the need to do so altogether.

When you renegotiate in advance, any initial irritation is short-lived and the relationship is, generally, unimpaired. What relationships sometimes lack is a degree of certainty, of dependability. If they know exactly what is expected and can depend on you to deliver, or inform them of a problem, they know how to plan their own work. If there is a change in circumstance, foreknowledge allows them to reschedule their own work accordingly, or to take whatever corrective action is necessary to optimise their position.

If no notice is given about a change in circumstances, it is likely that your colleague or your client will be left to deal with a difficult situation with very little flexibility available to them. You are much more likely to leave a poor, long-term impression than if you were honest about a possible delay or need to renegotiate.

I always impress upon suppliers that I would be far happier with a three-week delay of a critical piece of information or equipment by renegotiation, than a one day delay by default. The former gives me a framework in which I can adjust and therefore operate effectively. The latter shows me disrespect, and gives me little opportunity to adjust my plans. Of course, there are times when renegotiation is not acceptable to the person to whom you have made a commitment. When that occurs, you have a choice between honouring the commitment and maintaining the relationship, or breaking the commitment and risking the relationship. The choice is then based on relative priorities. You know what is important to you and the decision becomes easier to make.

CONCLUSION

A diary is one of the most powerful tools you have for focusing your daily activity, maintaining momentum on key areas of activity, acting flexibly and creating a positive attitude towards your performance.

Used properly, it harnesses energy to specific action strategies, designed directly to support your goals.

KEY MESSAGES FROM CHAPTER 11

■ *Choose a diary based on a format that works well for you, rather than purchase a diary or system based on marketing 'hype'. Ensure that it has adequate space to mark appointments and those commitments not based on a specific time.*

■ *Use pencil in your diary so that the daily plan made in advance of the day can readily be turned into a record of what actually occurred. Make sure that the record accounts for the major activities of the day, whether or not they feature in your time-line plan.*

■ *Use 'to do' lists if they work for you. Experiment with translating them to daily action commitments and only review the 'to do' list as part of your regular weekly action planning.*

■ *Be careful about the commitments you enter into. Know that if anything crops up that makes it unlikely for the commitment to be met, it is wise to renegotiate the commitment in advance of the due date. Do this with respect and understanding for those who are affected.*

CHAPTER 12

Making meetings work

Meetings are occasions where one person takes minutes and the others waste hours.

Meetings can be great time wasters and the time wasted usually derives from two principal sources: lack of planning and follow-up, and poor conduct of the meeting.

I have yet to meet a manager who has not complained about the amount of time he or she spends in meetings. The complaints are common: there are too many meetings; most of them are unnecessary; they go on far too long; most are a waste of time. Very few of the people who complain realise that the remedy lies in their own hands.

The fable of the emperor and his clothes is relevant here. All the citizens were used to the 'game' of doing what they were told until someone who knew too little came along to play the game. At that point everyone miraculously saw what had been obvious all along.

Challenge the meeting 'game' in your organisation. Accept that, for the most part, the amount of time you waste in meetings is your responsibility. Individually we have the power to radically reduce the time we spend in meetings and to improve the value of the meetings we do attend. Used effectively, with proper attention to the principles of focus already discussed, meetings can be harnessed to achieve results.

IS IT NECESSARY?

The first step to becoming more effective in relation to the meetings you attend is to decide whether the meeting, or your attendance, is really necessary. Perhaps it is possible to attend for a particular item of interest, rather than attend the entire meeting. All that is required is a conversation in advance with the person who has convened the meeting.

Too often calling a meeting is the result of indecisiveness. If this is a personal issue for you, bite the bullet and make a decision which lies in your own power rather than call a meeting on the pretence of consensus. If it is because too much power is retained centrally in your organisation, try pushing the barrier forward incrementally. Choose something not too contentious initially and then take more responsibility. Work towards being judged by results.

We also tend to call meetings or attend meetings out of habit. If you are thinking of convening a meeting always ask whether it is really necessary, and whether there is another more effective way of achieving the same outcome. If you are invited to attend a meeting, consider what purpose is served by attending. Consider also the outcome you expect, and how your attendance contributes to what is important to you. There may be no need to attend at all, or your needs may be served by attending for a particular issue. There may even be some other more efficient way of meeting your objective. A phone call or teleconference may be a more effective use of everyone's time; even a round-robin memorandum or using electronic mail facilities may achieve the same result.

Explore useful and effective ways of reaching your objective. The key element behind your decision will be to know what your purpose is. Clarity of focus is as important in the context of managing your time in relation to meetings as in any other. If your desired outcome is clear, the optimum way to achieve it will often be clear also.

Meetings are time consuming and very costly. There is the direct cost in wages or salaries and payroll on-costs for all participants, and the opportunity cost of the hours spent by each participant.

As a general rule, therefore, calling a meeting and attending a meeting is a last resort. If you can handle the issue in another way, without undermining any agreements you have in your organisation regarding information flow and consultation, do so.

WHAT KIND OF MEETING?

In deciding whether to call a meeting or whether to attend one, it is useful to know what kind of meeting it is meant to be. This is part of being clear about your intention towards the meeting. There are many different types of meetings. The most obvious is the meeting designed to make some form of group decision. Others that readily spring to mind include:

- brainstorming meetings designed to discover the widest range of action options prior to making a decision;
- consensus-forming meetings;
- information-dispensing meetings;
- meetings designed for particular negotiating purposes or for quasi-judicial or disciplinary purposes;
- performance review meetings;
- meetings for coordination and review;
- meetings for providing recognition and acknowledgement for achievement;
- meetings called specifically to reassure staff on their value in particular internal or external circumstances;
- business planning meetings; and
- budgetary review meetings.

Information regarding the general purpose of a meeting may be clear from the agenda. If it is not, you may want to inquire as to its general purpose. If you assumed that the purpose of the meeting was to make a decision and you find yourself in the middle of a brainstorming session, you may be justified in feeling quite annoyed. If you attend a meeting expecting to have a general discussion about planning options in your organisation and find general information being provided to a much wider group of people than anticipated, you may also feel annoyed.

Being clear about the type of meeting helps focus your attention on the outcome. It also helps you decide on the process to be followed in running the meeting. For example, a brainstorming meeting has quite different parameters to a standard informal business meeting.

When you are clear about what kind of meeting it is, and you are focused on you own outcomes in being there, time spent in meetings is likely to be that much more productive.

AGENDAS

The existence of an accurate agenda is an essential piece of information when deciding whether to attend all of the meeting or simply a part of it. It is also an essential element in properly preparing yourself to participate in a meeting. The agenda should be complete in itself and any portion for 'other business' minimised or eliminated entirely.

The agenda should clearly indicate the nature of each item, including what type of business item it is, along with any recommendations to consider. The agenda needs adequate information attached to it in order to enable participants to address each issue in the most time-efficient way. Agenda items should describe the context carefully, together with any limits on decision or discussion parameters.

In short, the agenda and its attachments should contain everything necessary for the people attending the meeting to reach a desired outcome. Anything short of this and you risk delays while further information is sought or additional consultation is made. If the agenda is complete, all participants have everything necessary for a successful outcome, as well as no excuse if they have not prepared themselves properly for the meeting.

The agenda should always be distributed sufficiently in advance to give all participants time to prepare for it, although occasionally it may be necessary to call a meeting with a degree of urgency. In these circumstances, everyone who attends should still have a clear idea of what the purpose is and why they are meeting. This may take the form of verbal advice or some other less formal advice about the discussion.

On balance, if you have to rush notice for a meeting, make your decision some other way. If people have no time to properly prepare, they are unable to contribute to the best of their ability. You waste their time and yours.

The preparation of an agenda is the first stage of convening a meeting. It is the beginning of the process designed to clarify what you want to achieve. Do this *before* you announce the meeting if possible. A good agenda is even more important for you as a participant. It is your first indication of the matters to be discussed and the beginning of your analysis as to whether to attend.

As a general rule, the fewer the number of agenda items the more effective your meeting will be. A large number of agenda items runs the risk of making the business under discussion range

182

too widely. This may necessitate drawing a greater number of participants to the meeting, 'just in case'. The end result for each participant is that the value of the time spent at the meeting is diminished considerably. My preference is for a meeting with a maximum of two or three agenda items.

The agenda should be precise about the date, time and place of the meeting. If you convene a meeting, arrange for your meeting room arrangements (booking, seating and any other meeting room aids) to be confirmed the day before.

PREPARING FOR YOUR MEETING

As a convenor, much of the necessary preparation for your meeting can be done simply by being as thorough as possible in preparing the agenda. Additional time may be spent on enlisting the attendance and support of obvious key players. If there is one person with a particularly vital role to play, you need to enlist his or her support in a way that does not alienate other participants. This is an issue-by-issue skill and the extent to which you operate in this area should be carefully balanced against the interests of building good working relationships.

Further preparation may involve providing additional information to meet the specific needs of one or more participants.

In addition you should spend ten to fifteen minutes close to the start of the meeting making sure your own focus is clear.

As a participant, your role is quite different. In many cases preparation begins when you have received your agenda papers. This may mean gathering additional information so your attitude about an item is clear, or consulting your associates so that their view is taken into account when forming your own. It may be that you need to speak with the convenor in order to clarify an aspect of the agenda or to make sure your attendance is required, why and for what agenda items.

There may need to be some research commissioned to fully understand the issue from your perspective, or advice and assistance sought from outside your department or organisation. In doing this you should take account of any confidentiality issues inherent in an agenda item.

Finally you should work out what is your desired outcome for the issue and decide the full implications of it for you. Consider how your position can be optimised in relation to the issue and what are the limits of an acceptable outcome.

Sometimes it is useful to assess the desired outcomes for the other participants and for the convenor. The best way to do this is to ask. Assess what areas of agreement there are and work out a way to minimise any potential conflict either before the meeting or during it.

If you decide you only want to be there for a portion of the meeting, check with the convenor that this is in order. You might also ask the convenor about the time the item is likely to be discussed and agree to your availability at that time.

Whether you are in the role of convenor or participant, the work you put into preparing for a meeting is high leverage activity. First, it gives you a focus on whether the meeting is really necessary. Once that has been established, preparation for the meeting itself streamlines your contribution to it. Do something to encourage others to act in the same way. Second, it provides a focus for what you have to say based on what is important to you; it should reduce your 'need' to speak on aspects of the discussion that do not directly concern you. Third, it also assists your focus on any necessary follow-up action that is relevant to you.

MEETINGS AND TIME

Planning and preparation are probably the most significant ways to prevent meetings racing away with time. This is because adequate time spent in planning and preparation and properly articulating outcomes or goals makes the other elements of the meeting work so much better.

There are two time-management techniques of great value in reducing the time wasted in meetings. First is getting a meeting off to a prompt start. Second is finishing it on time.

Starting on time

Starting a meeting on time is initially the responsibility of the convenor, although clearly all participants have a part to play. Most organisations I have observed start their meetings late. In some cases the 'average' time wasted is 15–20 minutes. In one work environment there was an unspoken 15 minute period of grace. This meant participants rarely arrived inside the 15 minutes and, more often, were late for the late start! Meetings habitually started 25–35 minutes after the scheduled time.

184

A meeting becomes even more of a time-waster and inconvenience when the convenor recapitulates key discussion for late-comers. The way through this morass of limiting, time-wasting practice is for you to *develop a reputation as someone who starts meetings on time and who refuses to reward any late-comers by recapitulating the discussion that occurred in their absence.*

Every time you wait for people to arrive and recapitulate for late-comers, you give two messages. First, to those who turned up on time, you indicate that their punctuality is unimportant to you. Second, you indicate that those arriving late are behaving acceptably. Your message 'punishes' punctual colleagues and rewards the tardy.

In my seminars I always get off to a prompt start. At the morning-tea break, however, I announce the current time and ask for agreement as to the time of resumption. If there is a room clock this is the reference time. I always start spot on time, even if half the audience is still wandering back into the room. I make no comment about lateness as I believe that as adults they are responsible for their own learning. This process is repeated at the luncheon and afternoon-tea breaks. It is amazing how many people respond and how quickly. If I were to moralise about the time it took to have them all back in the room, or to ignore the start time and wait until when they all returned, I would have had longer and longer to wait by the second and third breaks. I would be wasting my valuable time and that of those who were back in the seminar on time.

My commitment to my work is too important not to optimise the time I have with the people who attend my seminars. I am not prepared to waste the time of those who act as if their time with me is important. I was delighted during one seminar when one manager told me of her experience. She had attended a previous seminar of mine and arrived late. I had apparently made no comment and had not even appeared to notice her. She took this lesson back into her work environment: her sales meetings began to start on time and those who came late had to back up afterwards for essential information. She reported an enormous change of attitude to the meetings and was delighted at how her own time in meetings had become more valuable. She had even begun working on her own senior manager.

Finishing on time

Another aspect of convening a meeting is in having a clear idea at the outset of how long the meeting should take. What I recommend is building a set finishing time into your meeting *as part of your goal setting and planning for the meeting.*

Meetings always seem to take longer than people think they will. This is because they have ignored how well Parkinson's First Law applies to the conduct of meetings: 'Work expands so as to fill the time available for its completion', and 'a thing to be done swells in importance and complexity in direct ratio with the time spent'![1]

Even when we are meticulous about other aspects of planning for a meeting, the crucial aspect of how long the meeting should take is often ignored. I suggest that you make this aspect of your planning for meetings obvious. At the beginning of a meeting you will have an idea as to how long you expect it to take. In deciding this err on the cautious side; it is as well not to under-commit. Announce this at the beginning and reach agreement with the group about a specific finishing time.

During the course of the meeting, bring your meeting back on target by reminding everyone of the importance of the discussion outcomes. Do this in the context of the agreement to finish at a specified time. Focusing on action and time in this way has a salutatory effect. Try it and see how much easier it is to contain meetings within reasonable time limits. If you have a problem about getting your people thinking in this way, try commencing a one-hour meeting at noon with a view to completing it at the 1 p.m. luncheon break. Announce your own need to be away from the meeting at 1.00 p.m.

There are occasions when it may be thought necessary, even with a well conducted meeting, to exceed a time limit. My view is that it is best not to do so without checking with your colleagues whether it is appropriate. If a participant has so planned his or her day as to rely on leaving the meeting at a certain time, it may well be better to re-convene the meeting at a time when everyone can give the issue their undivided attention.

As a participant in a meeting you have a responsibility to the others in the meeting and to yourself in seeing that the meeting starts and finishes on time. To a large extent this depends on how you play the game in the conduct of the meeting. In general, your support for the convenor should be passive and cooperative rather than active. In some circumstances it may be appropriate for you to actively intervene to encourage the convenor to bring the meeting back into focus. If you have a concern about the way the convenor discharges this aspect of the role, it is far better to do this off the record after the event, so that next time the focus is clearer. If you have to intervene during a meeting, do so in a way that maintains good relationships with your colleagues. Above all be very cautious about damaging the authority of the convenor.

CONDUCT OF MEETINGS

Whether or not the strict rules of meeting procedure apply to a meeting depends on the relevant legal requirements or on convention. Formal procedure can be time consuming not to mention unnecessary for small meetings, and you might like to avoid them unless you have some legal responsibility to fulfil. On the other hand, some degree of agreed procedure makes good sense if you have to preside over a large heterogenous gathering. The focus here is to establish an effective practice for small business meetings where informality and expedition are the watch words.

Excessive informality can be time consuming. There is a nice balance to be created between the sense of ownership and commitment deriving from a freer procedure and from bringing a meeting to a satisfactory outcome within defined time limits. Clearly the key to productive informal meetings lies in the subtle way a convenor maintains the focus on issues and outcomes.

Conduct as convenor

Now that your preparation is complete, you have started on time and the meeting is under way, you as convenor have a responsibility to bring the items on the agenda to a conclusion. Introduce each agenda item by declaring what the anticipated outcome might be. This could be a suggested direction the discussion might take or a specially formulated recommendation for decision. Once this has been done, ensure that the discussion is directed to the topic. If discussion wanders off the point, gently and firmly return it to focus. There is always a dilemma as to how wide discussion is allowed to range. Too strict a rein on discussion may inhibit good ideas, while loose control wastes time and renders the discussion unproductive.

For some issues, there may be some guidelines or parameters within which they should be discussed. These guidelines should be stated at the outset and used as the basis for discussion.

As each discussion is completed, summarise the outcome and offer a trial resolution. If this excites further discussion, so much the better. It is a mark of a good convenor to be open to the signs of disagreement and allow people full expression. Often people who disagree in a discussion within a meeting simply want to have their disagreement heard; they would be most surprised to have it acted upon. The key as convenor is to ensure a balance is maintained between the opportunity to be heard and unnecessary discussion.

In a long discussion, it is useful to provide interim summaries, as this aids continued focus on the outcome. If you have framed a consensus, you may be able to bring it to a speedy resolution.

If one of your number cannot agree, it might be possible to proceed on the basis of a majority decision. When someone asks for a dissent to be recorded in a minute of a meeting, you probably have more of a problem than the unanimity of the specific decision. There is a strong likelihood of some deeper underlying issue that can be more fruitfully addressed outside the meeting. Sometimes, despite your careful planning at the outset, you may find it best to defer a decision for further discussion until a later time. This depends on how urgent the issue is and on the need to maintain good team relationships overall.

Be sure to be clear in your summary about the action to be taken as a result of the decision and who is responsible and by when.

As part of your firm, although subtle, discipline as convenor, it is always important not to belittle the participants in any way: no put-downs, no disparaging views, no sarcasm. If anyone behaves badly at the meeting, make a note and deal with him or her privately after the meeting.

Your role as convenor is one of encouragement and support in the interests of an effective, expeditious outcome. It is one of team building and of support for the better performers and encouragement and development for those who, for one reason or another, do not do so well. It is a role of great responsibility.

Conduct as participant

When participating in a meeting, your preparation will indicate what you have to say. It is sensible to limit your contribution to what is necessary for meeting that purpose. Concentrate your contribution on what you know and what is important to you. If you agree with a previous contribution, say so, but there is no reason for you to say why, particularly if it mirrors a previous contribution. Similarly, repeating a lost or partly lost argument adds little to discussion and irritates your colleagues. Say what you have to say, respond to any comment it excites and leave it at that.

If you are in any doubt about when to intervene, take your lead from your convenor. Write a note to the convenor to indicate your interest, and wait for an appropriate moment for your intervention with the convenor's support.

Outside your own direct contribution to the discussion, it is perfectly proper for you to remind the convenor that the business in hand is not being properly addressed and there is a consequent need to tighten the discussion. This should be done sparingly and in a caring and productive way. Remember, convenor and participants are all on the one team. Similarly, if you are in disagreement with a contribution to the discussion, make your comments with care. Address the issue and not the person. Leave the other person clear about your support for them as an individual and your ongoing belief in their value, even if you cannot agree with their views.

Support the convenor of the meeting in any way you think useful in order to bring the meeting to a successful conclusion, particularly if this means staying silent when you have nothing useful to contribute.

THE MINUTES OR ACTION RECORD OF A MEETING

For most meetings, there must be some form of 'official' note or minute taken which records decisions and any action agreed upon. If you have been assigned responsibility for this, there are a number of key principles to follow. The first of these is to write a first draft of the minutes immediately after the meeting. Your memory of the meeting will be far clearer and more subtle immediately afterwards, than even a few hours. Research tells us that after 24 hours some 80 per cent of the detail of our recall is lost. The most efficient way to record the minutes is to use a dictating machine, as this is easy to use and the draft of the record can be done very quickly. It does not matter how 'clean' the first draft is. What is important is that you get the minutes down on tape or paper as quickly as possible. There is time enough afterwards to finetune the result. Your minutes should be concise and to the point, covering the topic addressed, with an outline of the key elements of the discussion. They should detail all follow-up action, the person whose action responsibility it is, and when it is due.

The minutes should be completed and circulated as soon as possible after the meeting. I always aim for a 24-hour turn around. Prompt dispatch of the minutes presents action responsibilities to individuals in time for appropriate action to be taken.

If you are a participant it is a good idea to jot down your particular action responsibilities immediately after the meeting. If there is a day on which you know it is appropriate to act on one or other of them, put this directly into your diary. Otherwise, put the action folder into your re-submission drawer for the next weekly review of action. As soon as the official version of the minutes appears, check what you have recorded against them. If there is a discrepancy, check with the minute-taker or convenor.

CONCLUSION

Our behaviour in calling a meeting is our own responsibility. What we do about meetings we are invited to attend and the level of communication we adopt is also our responsibility.

Meetings properly used are enormously valuable. Used indiscriminately and without thought to their real cost, they can be a major source of poor performance that has a direct effect on motivation and profitability.

KEY MESSAGES FROM CHAPTER 12

- *Don't call a meeting unless it is necessary, and unless there is no other way to deal with the issue you want to address. Be certain also what kind of meeting you want and know that this reflects your desired outcomes for it.*

- *Don't attend a meeting to which you have been invited unless you judge it to be a valuable use of your time.*

- *When attending a meeting make sure you know precisely what it is you want to achieve by your participation. Without being inflexible, have a good idea of your expected outcomes of a meeting you attend.*

- *Make sure an agenda for a meeting contains all the information necessary for an informed decision. Make sure there are no surprises.*

- *If an agenda you receive is not complete, do your homework prior to the meeting; ask for additional information or opinion beforehand.*

- *Start and finish your meetings on time.*

- *Only contribute to a discussion at a meeting when what you say adds value to the discussion.*

- *Write up the minutes of the meeting immediately after the meeting. Write your own action steps deriving from the meeting as the meeting progresses.*

CHAPTER 13

Using information technology

The skills of personal focus and organisation, and the relationship skills of team leaders with working colleagues can be supported by the use of the rapidly growing range of information technology available. Many of us work in environments in which information technology supports the main business purpose of our organisation in a substantive way. This book would be incomplete if there were no discussion on this important aspect of our work.

A wealth of products exists in the world of information technology. There are the many mainframe and local area network systems providing computing power to multiple users over many sites, linking internal and external processing and communications. There are the notebook, laptop and standard personal computers, many of them with facsimile and other connective devices. At another level there is a multiplicity of electronic personal organisers with diary, project control and simple data storage functions, many with 'connectability' to other, more complex computing systems.

On the applications side, the variety is almost infinite. Name a need and someone, somewhere, will have written a program and perhaps marketed a product in response to that need. Applications range from the commonly used—the most universal being word processing—to spreadsheet analysis, simple database capacity and graphics. More sophisticated general productivity tools— such as electronic mail and diary systems, desktop publishing and complex project management—are now available on the simplest of home computers as the power of the micro processor increases.

192

Modem and other linkages for connecting word processing function to multiple facsimile output are also quite readily available.[1] More specialised applications apply to specific industries and professions—for example, knowledge-based systems and design and control tools, many of which require a fairly sophisticated processing capacity.

My purpose is not to traverse this complex territory in any substantial way, but to cover the way information technology issues can support the team and team leader in improving performance and realising potential.

IS IT WORTH IT?

There is no doubt that introducing information technology is high leverage activity. The power of computers is growing exponentially, with some new wonder available each day. The potential for productivity gains are considerable—so much so that the average team leader feels compelled to rush to a computer or information technology solution for a particular administrative or control 'problem'. Certainly my experience indicates that many senior managers, particularly those who have had only slight direct exposure to the technical aspects of information technology, often regard a computer solution as a universal panacea.

Before launching into the apparently obvious solution of information technology, therefore, it makes sense to consider:

1 whether there is not some simple, more efficient, low-cost mechanical alternative, and
2 whether the particular information technology solution answers the problem in an effective way.

For example, I still use a manual, although elaborate, diary and planning system. I have yet to find any form of computer application that provides the same portability, flexibility, ease and speed of access that my diary system provides.

In a similar vein I was fascinated to see, when on a consulting assignment with a large government department, that the use of electronic pocket organisers, of whatever brand, was confined to those senior staff who were previously rather poorly organised. Those who were generally well organised and who had sophisticated needs used manual diary systems.

More interesting still was that none of the many information technology professionals I met used electronic organisers. They

193

were all extremely well organised at a personal level and relied on simple manual diary systems, combined with the intermittent use of the nationally available electronic diary system, as part of the local area network-based electronic mail system.

This is no coincidence. The sophisticated, well-organised person will often find that the technology available today for personal diary systems is largely unsatisfactory. Now that much heralded notepad systems are readily available it may be a different story. These notepad systems are in effect an 'intelligent' pocket organiser, distinguished from the current technology by:

1 the capacity to enter data via handwriting onto a simple, highly portable screen;
2 their accessibility to more than one person; and
3 the capacity to enter shorthand notes in diary and reminder systems.

Just as effective manual diary systems are readily available, many 'databases' can be maintained manually. Simple card systems for service campaigns in customer relations may be more than adequate. Telemarketing call sequencing can be effectively established and maintained. Administrative control systems may be simpler and easier to operate quite effectively with a well-designed manual system.

Gerry Harvey of the Harvey Norman discount stores in Australia, for example, operates a business with a turnover of close to half a billion dollars without a central computer. Despite this (he would say because of it) he has finger-tip daily control statistics from all his 100 plus stores around the country.

The wider corporate costs of the purchase of hardware and software for a computer application are considerable. First, there are the often hidden costs of maintenance for hardware and software, not to mention data integrity. Second, and often poorly anticipated, there are the costs of staffing and training for the most effective use of the application throughout an organisation. Taken together these additional costs are often greater over a fairly short time frame than the initial outlay. Add in the costs of upgrades and the introduction of 'Trojan horse' applications related to the one you have specifically introduced and the exercise can become very expensive indeed. By this I mean application and packages which look complete in themselves until you find that, to be truly effective, they require a great deal of additional software or an upgrade of your computer.

The need to fully understand the properly costed benefits

against the full cost of the purchase is of paramount importance. The costing should include, in addition to the purchase price, amortisation and maintenance of hardware and software, staffing and training costs throughout the organisation over a three or five-year period, and the cost of your time and energy in selecting the most appropriate solution to your business needs. In assessing the benefits, direct and indirect costs should be included. Some notional figure should be given to any non-quantifiable benefits such as market positioning.

The majority of information technology solutions are fully justified and I am making no attempt here to suggest otherwise. My experience as a consultant tells me that there is a need to 'hasten slowly'; the first step in that process may well be to investigate the possibility of a simple and effective mechanical alternative.

Another major lesson I have learnt from my experience is to move towards information technology on the simplest possible statement of need. Most new applications tend to be vastly more sophisticated than is necessary in order to serve the underlying business need.

WORKING WITH PEOPLE

All computer systems are operated by people, whether you are introducing a system in a large operating environment or putting a desktop one in place in your own office. This means that some adjustment will have to be made to the flow of work related to the new system in order to ensure that the investment you have made in the technology provides the fullest possible benefit.

It is necessary, therefore, to consider what management and procedural systems you have to put in place to make it work most effectively. It may also be necessary to measure performance and productivity within your team and to measure your own effectiveness in new ways. Consider access to the data available on your new system. This may mean devising a way for decision makers affected by it to access the data or information, perhaps by modem device, or other forms of linkage to key people with whom you relate closely in your business.

Consider also the extent to which it is useful for you to connect to technology in the home: personal computers, touch-tone telephones, facsimiles, electronic mail, etc. There is a growing tendency for many people, either members of larger organisations or those running smaller cottage-based businesses, to work partly from home.

OVERALL CONGRUENCE—WORKING STYLE

Beyond making sure that the people aspect of your installation is properly managed, it is useful to ensure that whatever you do, whatever system you employ, the particular system is consistent with your way of operating. There is absolutely no point in introducing something into your environment 'to improve your productivity' if it is foreign to your normal way of operating. You may well become less effective as a result, or spend so much time becoming used to it, that it becomes totally disruptive and hence counter-productive. This could result in partial use of the new system which is wholly inefficient, given the size of your investment.

CHOOSING AN APPLICATION

There are traps in purchasing non-standard applications, by which I mean those products that are customised, or written or devised especially for your business needs.

Standard products, those made for a mass market and sold and supported nationally if not internationally, come with support systems and hot-line advisory services at a reasonable cost; this is not always so for non-standard applications. Standard applications are more often than not constantly being researched and refined and these developments are available to you at reasonable rates.

Applications bought off-the-shelf are normally substantially less expensive than custom-built or tailored applications. They provide compatibility among team members and with other teams or organisations with whom you have regular dealings.

On the other hand, I have seen special purpose or customised applications become so idiosyncratic to a particular user over time, that they became difficult or impossible to support as far as the original supplier was concerned. It is an expensive and energy-sapping exercise, and a lesson still to be learnt by many.

Be careful, in your analysis of alternative applications, that you are comparing like with like. Talk to some people who have a perspective on the marketplace and who have an understanding of what the various alternatives have to offer. Speak to suppliers on the basis of a prepared set of questions, asking the same questions of each.

There are a number of useful things to consider when selecting application software and related hardware:

1 Be clear about the real needs to be met by the application, separately identifying those that are essential and those that are highly desirable.
2 Decide how you will test the products as you research what to buy. Decide how to weigh the characteristics of the short list of products against your requirements.
3 Decide how you will assess the less tangible aspects of the competing products: support structure, maintenance costs and performance, machine response times and supplier viability.
4 Decide how you will assess how well your computer handles the new application. Decide also what the cost will be if there is a need for any upgrade in processing capacity.
5 Engage in a process that ensures that as many possible applications are reviewed. This may involve discussions with people with similar requirements to see what they have used and what the result has been. Be careful of the natural desire for people who recommend products in this way to champion their own decision. If you are looking for a common application such as word processing or spreadsheets, it may be sufficient to canvas a few 'market leaders'. If you assess these and find them wanting, look for a more suitable alternative. Do be wary, however, of the more esoteric or exotic brand names. Test them and the stability of the supplier in considerable detail.
6 Assess what links should exist between personal computing systems and the larger corporate system.
7 Ensure that appropriate guarantees are in place when you do decide on your application, so that remedies—and I mean genuine remedies—are available if the application fails to meet a specified requirement in some way.
8 Obtain advice from a lawyer with experience in the computer industry on the nature of the contract you sign with your supplier(s).

Despite the time-consuming and very intensive nature of the effort involved, you will find that the time and effort is well spent.

USING A CONSULTANT

It is probably more cost-efficient in the long run to bring in some well-qualified technical assistance when choosing a standard application and/or the equipment on which it is to run. This is so even for the small operator where cash flow may not be strong and where short-term cost issues might indicate otherwise.

Be careful to chose a consultant who is independent of any particular supplier, not always an easy task. Check around the marketplace quite thoroughly for consultants with a good reputation in the general area of your preferred application. Insist on talking to client referees of the consultant, asking, in particular, about the extent to which the consultant ensured that the client referee became fully self-sufficient and independent of the consultant.

A PERSONAL ORGANISATION SYSTEM

In looking for a system for personal organisation, focus on how well it translates planning into commitment to action, and how easy it is to update and use the information technology equivalent of the daily page of a diary. Every aspect of your electronic diary/organiser system should be focused on ensuring that each entry in the goal-setting and planning phases of your work is automatically committed to an action point on a specific day. This should occur without the need for double or triple entry; the data entry process at the planning stage include a decision on when particular aspects of the plan should happen.

Failing to ensure that this occurs means that all your good work in planning remains embedded in the memory of your planning notes. Action on essential elements of your business direction will rely too heavily on your memory or on your ability to go back into your planning file and sort out particular action steps on a regular basis.

CONCLUSION

Using information technology aids will be a valuable and profitable experience for you, if you carefully define your objectives and analyse the costs of implementing a new way of doing things against their likely advantages. The time and resources you have available to you will determine the benefits that accrue.

Failure to analyse your position properly may well lead to time and cost commitments you might otherwise have preferred to avoid. The difficulty is that, once the commitment to travel in this direction is made, it is often very difficult, sometimes impossible, to reverse your direction.

KEY MESSAGES FROM CHAPTER 13

- *Assess the basic need for an information technology application. There might be a simple mechanical way of doing the work at less cost.*

- *Undertake a full cost benefit analysis of any proposal and include costs of any wider hidden implications throughout the organisation.*

- *Consider the people involved in the new application. Consult with them fully about the need and the benefits. Train them thoroughly in the new equipment and involve them in the redesign of any related procedures. As far as practicable, ensure that the new system 'fits' with the culture in which it is to operate.*

CHAPTER 14

Conclusion

At the beginning of our journey together, I indicated that my purpose in writing this book was to support people in organisations in establishing, developing and maintaining:

- the skills of relationships with colleagues;
- an understanding of the nature of change and what it takes to encourage an ongoing commitment to change in a positive creative way; and
- the skills of personal organisation in support of their other roles.

My increasing concern is that the major focus of people's attention in businesses and in organisations of all kinds is on the technical tasks of their position. They are focused almost exclusively on the day-to-day rather than the longer term issues that are critical to their success. Stephen Covey[1] calls this [the antithesis of] 'Sharpening the Saw'—the habit we have of cutting wood with a blunt saw day after day, too busy to take time out to sharpen the saw and so save time and energy disproportionately greater than the time taken to sharpen it.

Chief among the longer term issues is that of building relationships among the people in our organisations. This key activity has three important dimensions. First, there is the need to support people in developing their personal sense of self-value and in valuing the contribution they are able to make to the organisation. Second is the need to support people in developing relationships with each other in work units and ad hoc teams. These are the relationships that ensure quality internal service as well as the client and customer service objectives of an organisation. Third is the need to support the relationships between the people of an organisation and the organisation itself, to involve them in the decision-making process in all areas where they are directly affected, and to encourage them to work towards a common purpose and vision.

These three areas of relationships, necessarily supplemented by full attention to the organisation's tangible outcomes, are the key building blocks of individual performance at the highest level, contributing significantly to the performance of the organisation as a whole. They are also the key building blocks in client or customer service, of continuous improvement in service and manufacturing processes, and of the creativity and flexibility essential for responding to the rapidly changing world in which we live. They are the building blocks of team building and of the learning organisation that is encouraged by true leadership.

The new organisation of the 21st century requires flatter organisational structures with fewer middle managers and greater emphasis on the people close to the cutting edge. Old notions of control and of detailed accountability do not have the same value in our rapidly changing world. Flexibility of response and the capacity of people to think and act on their own initiative are becoming more and more important. We need to provide an environment in which the skills of leadership are encouraged and rewarded at all levels of our organisations.

To exhort readers to spend more time on the relationship skills of their role while maintaining their focus on their tangible outcomes is, of itself, unreasonable. After all, the new century and its people will demand more flexibility, more time spent with family and in leisure and recreational pursuits, not less. This is why I have combined an emphasis on relationships, and the skills of working with colleagues, with the techniques of creating and maintaining focus. This is also why I have emphasised the twin skills of leadership—the skills of personal resource management and focus, and the skills of relationships with colleagues—and the way this can be harnessed in working with other people.

Throughout the book I have stressed the need to do things differently; to be open to new ways of looking at an issue. I have pointed to ways of developing the freedom to act proactively, anticipating relevant change, and adapting and adjusting to likely new demands rather than reacting to change as a matter of simple survival. Indeed, in many instances I have offered tips on to how to create and maintain change.

I have included a substantive section dealing with the nature of the change process itself and what we as individuals and as part of an organisation may do to adapt to work place demands as painlessly and productively as possible.

The title of this book, *Leading from Within*, indicates my confidence that we all have the ability to make the changes necessary for higher levels of personal and team performance, and to do so in a way that provides the joy and happiness that derive from real achievement.

Leading from Within is about being responsible for the results you obtain as you live your life. It is about respect for people; it is about trust and commitment. It is also about how personal integrity and choice are the very essence of the relationships we have with ourselves and our colleagues.

I often end my seminars by telling a story I read in 1990 on the front page of the now defunct Sydney newspaper *The Daily Mirror*. It is about the boxer, Jeff Fenech. In 1984, at the Olympic Games in Los Angeles, he gained a majority of the referees' decisions in the [gold medal] final of the bantamweight division. The decision was overruled by the tournament umpire and Fenech was extremely upset to say the least. At the depths of his despair he was given a piece of paper with some verse written by Nancye Simms on it. The story in the paper said that Fenech has since carried the paper with him through numerous professional fights leading to three world championships. I do not think there is anything that better encapsulates the sense of what I have sought to achieve in *Leading from Within* than this verse.

> Winners take chances.
> Like everyone else, they fear failing,
> but they refuse to let the fear control them.
> Winners don't give up.
> When life gets rough, they hang in
> until the going gets better.
> Winners are flexible.
> They realise there is more than one way
> and are willing to try others.
> Winners know they are not perfect.
> They respect their weaknesses
> while making the most of their strengths.
> Winners fall, but they don't stay down.

They stubbornly refuse to let a fall
keep them from climbing.
Winners don't blame
fate for their failures
nor luck for their successes.
Winners accept responsibility
for their lives.
Winners are positive thinkers
who see good in all things.
From the ordinary, they make
the extraordinary.
Winners believe in the path they
have chosen even when it's hard
even when others can't see
where they are going.
Winners are patient.
They know a goal is only as worthy
as the effort that's required to achieve it.
Winners are people like you.
They make this world a
better place to be.

Nancye Simms

Let me conclude by saying that I have a vision for a world in which the dreams and performance of individuals are stimulated and developed for the benefit of all people . . . in which honesty and openness of intent and practice prevail . . . in which the process of nurturing, accepting and appreciating the worth of oneself and others, and of treating oneself and others in a way one would wish to be treated, flourish and . . . in which people are willing to take a stand and to be judged by it.

If I have taken one reader further towards this vision I shall be well satisfied.

Notes

INTRODUCTION

1 Henry Ford, *Today and Tomorrow*, Doubleday, 1926.
2 And surely today he would extend this to include service and delivery processes.

CHAPTER 1   Focused attention for personal success

1 The study was conducted in 1985 with personal success measured in purely financial terms.
2 Teleology is knowledge of the *telic* or objective. We humans do nothing without deciding consciously or subconsciously what the end point or goal of our thought or action is to be.
3 There are numerous stories of people who have made radical changes and apparently beaten their particular life sentence. See particularly Ian Gawler, *You Can Conquer Cancer*, Hill of Content Publishing, Melbourne, 1984; Bernie Siegel, *Love, Medicine and Miracles*, Arrow Books, New York, 1986; and Ainslie Mears, *Life Without Stress*, Greenhouse, Melbourne, 1987.
4 Nomenclature is a hurdle for many. Major business goals are called 'strategies' in some planning environments in which I have worked. Specific action steps are strategies in others. Whatever the nomenclature, being clear about the nature of the hierarchy is important. If nomenclature *is* a problem for you, try a numeric distinction: level 1, 2 and 3 goals, objectives or strategies.
5 See Jane Elizabeth Allen, *Beyond Time Management—Organising the Organisation*, Addison Wesley Publishing, Reading, Mass., 1986.

6 The underlying principles of this chapter, on personal goal setting are also common to the business-planning process covered in chapter 2.

7 For more on this theme read Deal and Kennedy, *Corporate Cultures*, Penguin, London, 1988.

8 For an interesting discussion on the value of dignity in human relations see Edward de Bono, *The Happiness Purpose*, Penguin, Hammondsworth, 1979.

9 Patterns of behaviour build up within an organisation just as they do in the home. We become used to a certain behaviour in our colleagues and we develop subconscious patterns to deal with them.

10 Zig Ziglar, *GOALS: Setting and Achieving Them on Schedule*, Nightingale-Conant Audio, Chicago, 1988.

11 A good book with an excellent chapter on setting goals is Edwin A Locke and Gary P Latham, *GOAL SETTING: A Motivational Technique that Works*, Prentice Hall, New Jersey, 1984.

12 See chapter 10 on 'Action planning—organising your day' and chapter 11 on 'Using your diary' for strategies that will bring this into full effect. See also chapter 2 on 'Focused attention for organisational success' for techniques on breaking down a goal into action steps.

13 Susan Jeffers, *Feel the Fear and Do It Anyway*, Arrow Books, London, 1987, is an excellent work on dealing with fear.

14 See Napoleon Hill *Think and Grow Rich*, Fawcett Crest, New York, 1960.

15 There are literally innumerable references available on the effect of creative visualisation on high performance. See particularly Maxwell Maltz, *Psycho-Cybernetics*, Pocket Books, New York, 1969, and Napoleon Hill, *op cit*. Hill's book was first published in 1927 and is still on the best-seller lists!

16 Being unclear about goals and values at a personal level, coupled with poor communication with your environment about your goals and values, is a major contributor to overcommitment, an inability to say 'no', and a sense of drift which contributes so much to stressfulness.

CHAPTER 2 Focused attention for organisational success

1 Other key elements are: the competence of individuals in their allotted tasks; the extent to which individuals are valued for the part they play in the organisation and how this translates into willingness to extend oneself within the organisation; and finally, the way people at all levels relate to one another.

2 Two excellent books on the business planning process are Michael E Porter, *Competitive Strategy*, The Free Press, New York, 1980, and Michael E Porter, *Competitive Advantage*, The Free Press, New York,

1985. As the titles suggest they are set in the context of planning for competitive advantage.

3 See Robert J Kreigel and Louis Patler, *If It Ain't Broke . . . Break It!* Warner Books, New York, 1991, and Tom Peters, *Thriving on Chaos*, MacMillan, London, 1988.

4 Just as there are interesting discussions and misunderstandings about nomenclature in the planning literature, there are interesting 'chicken and egg' discussions about vision and goals. Do you devise your vision after you know what your goals are, or the reverse? In my view the answer is clear. The overall vision, or statement of principal purpose, is an essential prerequisite to the detail which brings it into effect. The 'confusion' only exists in ongoing businesses where the real sense of purpose has been lost or artificially imposed from above.

5 See Wilfred Jarvis, *Four Quadrant Leadership—Managers Manual* Sixth Edition, Wilfred Jarvis & Associates, Sydney, 1994, for the best and most complete study of this essential relationship.

6 Tony Buzan, *Use Both Sides of Your Brain*, A Dutton Paperbacks, New York, 1974, and *Make the Most of Your Mind*, Pan Books, London, 1977. Mind mapping has many other advantages. Used in small teams for task definition and planning in this way, it is a great team builder. It assists greatly in 'ownership' and delegation. I have also found mind mapping an important aid to memory. I use it in taking lecture notes as it makes a far more concise and accurate record.

7 The use of computers in tracking projects is invaluable for projects for which software is readily available or can be easily adapted. In their absence, the old-fashioned diary is very flexible; see Chapter 11 'Using your diary'.

CHAPTER 3 Staying on track 1

1 Mehrebian and Ferris, 'Influence of attitudes from new verbal communication in two channels' in *The Joural of Counselling Psychology*, vol. 31, 1967, pp. 248–52.

2 See particularly Genie Z Laborde, *Influencing With Integrity*, Syntony Publishing, Palo Alto, California, 1983.

3 The choice of words is deliberate. Mimicking is demeaning, mocking and counter-productive.

4 The reason for this is now clear to me. We absorb words at a far greater pace than anyone can speak them. Once we understand, or think we understand what is being communicated, we 'tune out', and focus on solutions, responses or something else altogether.

5 Alan Lakein, *How to Get Control of Your Time and Your Life*, Signet, New York, 1973.

6 Delegation, however, is not dumping. It is an art directed at improving your productivity and developing your people; see chapter 5 on

'Building a team of champions' and chapter 9 on 'Developing your team through delegation'.

7 C Northcote Parkinson, quoted from *Parkinson's Law and Other Studies in Administration*, Ballantyne Books, New York, 1957.

CHAPTER 4 Staying on track 2

1 To follow this argument in a more general way see Albert Ellis, *A New Guide to Rational Living*, The Wiltshire Book Company, North Hollywood, 1975, and Tom Miller, *The Unfair Advantage*, The Unfair Advantage Corporation, New York, 1993. Both books in quite different ways describe the major irrational thinking styles, with ways to direct your thinking more productively.

2 M Scott Peck, *The Road Less Travelled: A New Psychology of Love, Traditional Values, and Spiritual Growth*, Simon and Schuster, New York, 1978.

3 Martin E P Seligman, *Learned Optimism*, Random House Australia, Sydney 1992.

CHAPTER 5 Building a team of champions

1 Tom Peters and Nancy Austin, *A Passion for Excellence: The Leadership Difference*, Fontana Collins, Glasgow, 1985.

2 For information on the techniques of communication, see chapters 3 and 4 on 'Staying on track'.

3 When Gary Player chipped in from off the green to win a major golf tournament, a commentator remarked how lucky Player was. Player is said to have replied, 'Yes, and I've noticed that the more I practice the luckier I get!'

4 Communication with integrity ensures congruence between what you say and the more important messages you communicate by voice, expression and body language. The 'technology' of communicating with integrity is dealt with in a number of books, tapes and seminars. Among the most important is Genie Z Laborde, *Influencing with Integrity—Management Skills for Communication and Negotiation*—Syntony Publication, Palo Alto, California, 1983.

5 See Peter M Senge, *The Fifth Discipline—The Art and Practice of the Learning Organisation*, Doubleday, New York 1990.

6 They apply equally to family and other close relationships, to social, sporting and recreational activities that involve the active participation of other people.

7 Of great significance also is having your team members in the right position and ensuring that their productive skills are as focused as their motivation.

8 Fear of rejection is one of our most dominant fears, and the one each

of us working in a sales environment has to overcome in order to be truly successful.

9   Wilfred Jarvis, *Four Quadrant Leadership—Managers Manual Sixth Edition*, Wilfred Jarvis & Associates, Sydney, 1994.

10   University of Maryland, 1980.

11   *Stand and Deliver*, a Warner Brothers Film, starred Edward James Olmos and Lou Diamond Phillips, and was released in 1988.

12   The definition of 'rational' I use is the one used by Albert Ellis in his works on rational emotive therapy, principal among them being '*A New Guide to Rational Living*', The Wiltshire Book Company, 1975. Rational human activity is directed to two major goals. The first is surviving or remaining alive. The second is remaining *happily* alive, with a maximum of joy, pleasure, self-fulfilment, and a minimum of needless pain, dissatisfaction, discomfort and self-defeat.

13   Kenneth Blanchard and Spencer Johnson *The One Minute Manager*, Fontana Collins, Great Britain, 1983.

14   A lot has been written about appraisal schemes and there will be a lot more written. You may find a book edited by Russell Lansbury on the subject useful, *Performance Appraisal*, Macmillan, South Melbourne, 1981.

CHAPTER 6   The nature of change

1   Compare this with the Confuscian concept of crisis in which there are two components: catastrophe and challenge. The way we regard an adverse event (change)—as either catastrophe or challenge—is our choice.

2   Tom Miller, *The Unfair Advantage*, The Unfair Advantage Corporation, New York, 1993.

CHAPTER 7   Leading change in self

1   Subsequently published in *The Journal of General Psychology*, vol. 59, issue no. 1, pp 35–49, 1958.

2   Albert Ellis, *Reason and Emotion in Psychotherapy*, Citadel Press, Secaucus, New Jersey, 1962.

3   Albert Ellis, *A Guide to Rational Living*, Prentice Hall, New York, 1961.

4   Albert Ellis and Robert A Harper, *A New Guide to Rational Living*, Wilshire Book Company, North Hollywood, California, 1975.

5   Tom Miller, *The Unfair Advantage*, The Unfair Advantage Corporation, New York, 1993.

6   Martin E P Seligman, *Learned Optimism*, Random House Australia, Sydney, 1992.

7   See Walter Anderson, *The Greatest Risk of All—Why Some People Take Chances that Change Their Lives And Why You Can Too*, Houghton Mifflin, Boston, 1988, in which he describes the greatest risk of all as the ability to know oneself and to act on that knowledge.

8 M Scott Peck, *A World Waiting to be Born*, Bantam Books, New York, 1993.

9 See Erik Oleson, *12 Steps to Mastering the Winds of Change*, Macmillan, New York, 1993.

10 Morris West, *Shoes of the Fisherman*, William Heinemann, London, 1963.

CHAPTER 8 Leading change in others

1 M Scott Peck, *A World Waiting to be Born*, Bantam Books, New York, 1993.

2 Peter M Senge, *The Fifth Discipline—The Art and Practice of The Learning Organisation*, Doubleday, New York, 1990.

3 Wilfred Jarvis, *Four Quadrant Leadership—Managers Manual*, Sixth Edition, Wilfred Jarvis & Associates, Sydney, 1994.

4 James M Kouzes and Barry Z Posner, *Credibility: How Leaders Gain and Lose It, Why People Demand It*, Jossey-Bass, San Francisco, 1993.

5 Peter Block, *Stewardship—Choosing Service over Self-Interest*, Berrett-Koehler, San Francisco, 1993.

6 M Scott Peck, *The Different Drum*, Rider Paperbacks, London, 1987, and *A World Waiting to Be Born*, Bantam Books, New York, 1993.

7 Wilfred Jarvis, *op. cit.* Jarvis puts 'Empathy' between 'Neutrality' and 'Identification' on a continuum he calls the 'Leader's Energy Focus', ranging from 'Hostility' through 'Neutrality' and 'Empathy' to 'Identification'.

8 Alfie Kohn, *The Brighter Side of Human Nature*, Basic Books, Harper Collins, New York, 1990.

9 R Fisher and S Brown, *Getting Together*, Houghton Mifflin, Boston, 1988, referred to in Kouzes and Posner. *op cit.*

10 Peter Block, *The Empowered Manager*, Jossey Bass, San Fransisco, 1990.

11 James A Belasco, *Teaching the Elephant to Dance, The Manager's Guide to Empowering Change*, Plume Books, New York, 1990.

12 Stephen Covey, *The 7 Habits of Highly Effective People—Restoring the Character Ethic*, The Business Library, Melbourne, 1990.

13 M Scott Peck, *The Different Drum, op. cit.* and *A World Waiting to be Born, op. cit.*

14 James A Belasco, *op. cit.*

15 Quoted in a letter to the author in Walter Anderson, *The Greatest Risk of All* Houghton Mifflin, Boston, 1988.

16 James M Kouzes and Barry Z Posner, *op. cit.*

17 Ed Oakley and Doug Krug, *Enlightened Leadership—Getting to the Heart of Change*, Simon & Schuster, New York, 1991.

CHAPTER 9 Developing your team through delegation

1 See Chris Argyris, 'Good communication that blocks learning', *Harvard Business Review*, July–August 1994, pp. 77–85.
2 See again Wilfred Jarvis, *Four Quadrant Leadership—Managers Manual*, Sixth Edition, Wilfred Jarvis & Associates, Sydney, 1994.
3 Kenneth Blanchard and Spencer Johnson, *The One Minute Manager*, Fontana Collins, Great Britain, 1983.
4 Ayn Rand, *Atlas Shrugged*, Random House, New York, 1957.

CHAPTER 10 Action planning—organising your day

1 And one reflected also in Martin Seligman, *Learned Optimism*, Random House Australia, Sydney, 1992.

CHAPTER 12 Making meetings work

1 C Northcote Parkinson, quoted in *Parkinson's Law and Other Studies in Administration*, Ballantyne Books, New York, 1957.

CHAPTER 13 Using information technology

1 A modem connects two or more computer systems via the public telephone system on private voice networks.

CHAPTER 14 Conclusion

1 Stephen R Covey, *The 7 Habits of Highly Effective People*, The Australian Business Library, Melbourne, 1990.

Index

211